# WorkÍn Cryꞏ

## By ShÍrley o'Donoghue

*www.capallbann.co.uk*

# Working With Crystals

ISBN 186163 191X

Cover design by Paul Mason

Published by:

Capall Bann Publishing
Auton Farm
Milverton
Somerset
TA4 1NE

# Working With Crystals

# A Practical Guide

In your endeavour to become enlightened, to know your SELF, you lean on methods, rituals, crystals and a multitude of crutches.

While they may be educational in their own way, and provide occasion to play, they are in truth diversions.

When you, however, TRULY desire to be in light of your self, then you will drop your crutches and focus on the most dazzling crystal of all.

The Christ the YOU are.

Extract from *Garden of the Gods* - Peter O. Erbe.

By the same author, also published by Capall Bann:

Working With Natural Energy

# Contents

# Chapter 1

# What Is Crystal Healing?

Crystal Healing or Therapy can be traced back as far as Egyptian times but also some believe that it is linked to the ancient, mythical, lost city of Atlantis. What is known for sure is that countless civilizations have valued the use of crystals for their therapeutic benefits and have incorporated them in their religious and power rituals in order to harness the energies of the crystals. Even in our urban 'advanced' civilization, crystals and gems play a part. In churches the alter usually has items studded with precious gems and even our Royal Family, who own and wear countless items of jewellery on a daily basis surpass themselves when it comes to incorporating the Crown jewels into the ritual of the ascension to the throne. These are indeed symbols of power. The Ebers Papyrus tells us of the medicinal uses that crystals were put to in Ancient Egypt and gives illustrations of how various crystals were ground into powders in order to be ingested or used externally to aid particular ailments, there is also mention of crystals in the Bible.

As we have moved into the New Age, a renewed awareness of crystals and their healing properties have prompted a growth in interest in this ancient therapy. But, this is an interest where time has to be taken in order that one can fully comprehend and become aware of just what they do and how they work.

The following are four crystal healing descriptions which are all valid but place different emphasis on the therapy:

Science is beginning to catch up with the knowledge contained within different civilizations and religions regarding the subtle energy systems we all have. Modern science now acknowledges this as an electro-magnetic field or vibration.

1. Crystal Healing is an ancient method of healing which can be traced back to Eyptian times and beyond. It aligns the energy system of the body by using the piezioelectrical impulses that emanate from crystals to rebalance the electromagnetic field of the human body.

2. Crystal Healing works by drawing upon the properties of various crystals to enhance the bodys natural healing abilities.

3. Crystal Healing works by realigning mind, body and spirit using crystalline energy to facilitate a connection between the Universe and Earth.

4. A crystal is a chemical compound and nothing else. It has inherent orderliness and the ability to adjust to changes in its environment. It has inherent stability and at the vibrational level will maintain a constant electromagnetic pattern. The human body on the other hand is a composed of hundreds of thousands of different compounds within the actual physical body, the cells contain DNA which encompasses thousands of molecules as well as other proteins, enzymes, internal structures and organs. Each part has differing electrical charges and biomagnetic fields, which combine to make up a large and complex system.

Imagine the body as a large orchestra with millions of instruments (vibrational rates), using the same basic score (DNA) but following different parts (the functions of cell, organ systems), playing without stopping for 50, 60, 70 years. Over time we could imagine some players giving up altogether, some getting bored and changing the notes they use, some getting out of tune and others losing their place or reading someone elses part. Essentially, when the body picks up stress (some outside influence, good or bad, which alters the functioning of the whole system), it is like one instrument going slightly off key or falling behind by a note or two  a disharmony enters the system. The more disharmony there is, the harder it gets for the remaining instruments to stick to the score in front of them. Into this potential cacophony of vibrational rates, bringing a crystal is like striking a tuning fork. One single, pure tone is constantly emitted with no change, no variation and this acts as a guide by which a retuning can occur that reasserts local harmony (From *Crystal Doorways* by Simon Lilly).

Generally when receiving a Crystal Therapy treatment the recipient should be fully clothed and can either be sitting up or lying down. Crystals are usually placed around the body and occasionally on it. (Crystal Therapists usually work with couches that are a good few inches wider than the normal massage/therapy couch in order that they have enough space on the couch to place crystals around the body). The recipient can also hold a crystal. Many Crystal Therapists believe that we have a receiving and giving hand. It is worthwhile to take the time to see if this is the case for you. For most people, it seems that the left hand is the receiving and the right hand the giving. Explore which hand feels right holding the crystal. You many find that one hand is more sensitive to the energy of the crystal which can sometimes be felt by some individuals as an increase or decrease in temperature or a slight tingling or buzzing sensation in the hand which can occasionally be felt moving through the wrist and along the arm. This is perfectly normal!

Working with crystals usually induces a state of deep relaxation. People report an increased sense of well being and are sometimes aware of the crystals connecting energetically with their biomagetic field, which surrounds the body sometimes known as the aura.

Most Crystal Therapists believe that the foundations for physical illness are laid within this energy field that can encompass the mental, emotional or even spiritual aspects of the personality as well as the physical. When one or two or even all of these are out of balance over a long term period due to factors such as poor diet, the inability to release or resolve negative thought patterns, relationships etc. or when a shock or trauma is received the impact may then be sufficient for the dis-ease to manifest in the physical thereby creating illnesses. Medical science is beginning to accept this process and doctors generally feel that the onset of a serious illness can, in some cases, be traced back to a traumatic event 2 or 3 years prior. For a more definite illustration of this one only has to look at the physical toll that long term stress can exact upon the body in terms of the illnesses that are created such as high blood pressure, heart attacks, back problems etc. Illnesses that occur because the needs of the mental, emotional or even spiritual aspects of the person have either been ignored or not met.

In the years that I have been involved in the teaching of this subject, I have noticed that the changes that Crystal Therapy have brought about for many people are subtle but life enhancing. However, its worth noting at this point that Crystal Therapy does not take the place of conventional medical diagnosis and treatment for this you should always see your G.P. What Crystal Therapy can do, is act in a complementary way to support the  body's own natural healing ability in conjunction with conventional medical treatments.

Connecting with the energetic qualities held within a crystal is not as weird and wacky as it seems. Science has already identified that the piezioelectrical charge held within clear quartz crystals can be harnessed in order to provide energy to run computers, clocks etc and indeed it is possible to 'grow' manmade crystals using natural seeding crystals for these purposes.

The man-made crystals usually have the appearance of being almost too perfectly clear, a little like glass and I would say that in my opinion, they do not have the same qualities as natural crystal as they have not evolved naturally, over millions of years, although others may disagree, citing the factor that they are not subject to the karmic and or environmental implications of being attached to the earth.

Cheaper ranges of jewellery usually incorporate man-made gems such as cubic zircon which has a similar appearance to diamond etc.

These manmade quartz crystals are not to be confused with the Austrian or Lead crystals which are usually faceted to catch and reflect the light. Often used in Feng Shui to contain and generate the chi energy within a room, they are usually hung from a window and some pendulums are made from them also. Whilst they are very pretty to look at they are not considered by most crystal therapists to hold the same the therapeutic qualities of quartz although it should be noted that they contain elements of silica and lead.

On a daily basis we come into contact with crystals without even realizing it. The toothpaste that we use to brush our teeth contains a crystal called Fluorite, increasingly, liquid quartz is being used to fill cleansed tooth cavities and white bread contains Selenite for example. In addition to this we have an inbuilt crystalline structure in the physical body including cell salts, fatty tissue, lymphs red and white cells, thymus and pineal gland. Although identified by modern medicine these systems have not been properly explored.

Guradas explains the basis of crystal therapy thus:

*The internal workings of the ethers, which are forces that travel slightly faster than the speed of light, amplify energy that passes through a crystalline pattern. When the life force of vibrational remedies passes through a crystalline pattern, there is a slight amplification from a temporary expansion of mass than transpires as the energy approaches the speed of light. The proper of amplification creates more stability in energy. The crystalline pattern also stores electromagnetic energy and amplifies thought projections.*

*The pineal gland is a crystalline structure that received information from the soul, higher self, and subtle bodies, particularly the astral body. The subtle bodies often act as filters for teachings from the soul and higher self. From the pineal gland information travels to the right portion of the brain. If there is a need to alert the conscious mind to this higher information, it passes through the right brain in the form of dreams. Then the left brain analyzes it to see if the information can be grasped. This often occurs with clear dreams that offer messages. From the left brain information travels through the neurological system, specifically passing through two critical reflex points - the medulla oblongata and the coccyx. There is a constant state of resonance along the spinal column between these two points. Then the information travels to other parts of the body through the meridians and crystalline structures already described. The life force of vibrational remedies activates this entire procedure. This is a key process the soul uses to manifest karma in the physical body.*

Taken from '*Flower Essence And Vibrational Healing*' By Guradas Cassandra Press

6

# Choosing Crystals

*Beginning to work with crystals can appear to be daunting and it can initially seem easier to ask someone, more experienced in this therapy to choose which crystals would be of most benefit to you. This is wrong as the best person to choose a crystal for you, is you!*

Many people, when confronted by a wide selection of crystals will find that their eye is naturally drawn to a particular crystal. As crystals are quite tactile, it will usually be the first one that you are tempted to pick up or touch. You may be able to justify it logically by saying that it is your favourite colour or there is something about the shape but the logical justification of your choice is largely immaterial. It is the *intuitive* choice, which is the most relevant. It is possible to read about the qualities in books that particular crystals hold but this is always the qualities of a crystal that they the author has been able to access and may not be the same as the qualities that you can connect with. This is the most difficult aspect to take on board when working with crystals namely that you are the person most able to understand just what benefits the crystal can offer you. It is all too easy to dismiss your perceptions as imagination. You may find an author or teacher who you 'resonate' with and you will discover then that you will have a common agreement on the uses for a particular crystal. Just as easily you may find that you cannot accept another person's description. Both are valid and relevant but only to the individual. When in doubt, always pay attention to your first instincts.

It is possible to "confirm" your intuition by dowsing with pendulums, passing your hand over the crystal to see if you can feel and energetic connection which may manifest as heat, coolness, a drawing sensation or tingling, closing your eyes and choosing one or just asking for the right one to be shown before you enter the shop – when you do this it is usually the first one your eye is drawn to. Once you have chosen your crystal, it may be possible to refer to a particular author that you feel an affinity with and often you find that the author will confirm the aptness of your choice rather than reading up before you choose the crystal to see what you "should" have. Equally when choosing a crystal for someone else, try to hold a picture of that person in your mind whilst you make the selection. It is possible to refer to birthstone charts when all else fails but these charts can vary the selection of stones for each birthdate.

## Cleansing Crystals

Once you have chosen your crystal, it is important to cleanse them. Not in the accepted sense of the word, although you may wish to do this, but to cleanse them energetically of any negative influences or vibrations, to coin a new age phrase which they have picked up on their journey to you.

Crystals are usually mined by exploding them out of the earth, they are then frequently 'cleaned' by placing them in acid. Finally, they have to travel from miner to exporters, wholesalers to retailers where they are then at the mercy of anyone who chooses to connect with them by looking at or touching them. Each connection made with a crystal has an impact, either negatively or positively, upon the energetic qualities that it holds. Therefore a process of cleansing has to take place in order that these impacts are removed from the crystal and you can connect and work safely with it.

There are many tried and tested methods that people use for cleansing crystals. The most commonly used are also the most simple. I would suggest that you use the ones that appeal to you but do not feel that the quicker and simpler are less valid. Below are listed a few that you can work with but if you feel that you would prefer to use other methods do. However, always check that the process will not harm the crystal some crystals have a softer surface and can be scratched more easily whilst others do not respond well to being immersed in water. It is usually best to check with your retailer if you are unsure. For this reason I usually avoid using salt water because salt is also crystalline and it is possible to scratch softer crystals with salt but also when diluted in water, it can leave a residue on the crystal once the water solution has evaporated

## Suggested Methods For Cleansing Crystals

1. Holding the crystal under running water and visualizing the negative energy within it being washed away.

2. Using smoke from a candle, incense stick or smudge stick to cleanse the crystals by allowing the smoke to flow around the crystal.

3. Spraying with a Flower Essence such as Bach Flower Remedies but look out for other makes which are said to be extremely effective, such as Green Man Tree Essences or Healing Herbs for example.

4. Simple visualization, taking a few moments whilst holding the crystal to see the crystals negative energy being removed.

5. Leaving the crystals in a garden, out in the elements until you instinctively feel that the crystals are cleansed. However, dont forget to check for contra-indications, for example an Amethyst or Fluorite crystal will fade if left out in bright sunshine and Pyrite or Hematite will rust.

6. Using sound to cleanse them. This can be done by using Tibetan singing bowls or drums if you have them or simply by clapping your hands with the intent that the crystals are cleansed. You can also place them by music and allow the music to do the work. Bach or Handal are recommended for this but not heavy metal or rock music!

If you wish you can check the effectiveness of your cleansing rituals by using the pendulum before and after the process to see if you have effected a change in the crystal's energy. They can be cleared as often as you wish. Trust your instincts and when you find a crystal looking dull or the thought occurs to you just go ahead and clear them.


## Dedicating Crystals

Once you have cleansed the crystal, it is always a good idea to ensure that the crystal is dedicated or programmed to work in the purest and highest way. Crystals are, in many ways neutral tools, which we can activate, and request to work in any way that we wish.

This means that crystals can be used for positive purposes, of course, but it also follows that we can activate them to work for us in negative ways as well. Sometimes, when we find it difficult to see the 'bigger picture' we may be manipulating the crystal to work against universal law without realizing it. An example of this is when using them for healing, we may wish to provoke a strong reaction upon our patient in order to satisfy our ego whilst it may be more appropriate and in keeping with the needs of the patient not to feel anything at all at that point! On a more negative note, we may wish to manipulate others in order to 'punish' them for something they have done to us or to control them to do what *we* want rather than again abide by what is appropriate to the Higher Self of the individual. I therefore always ask that my crystals be dedicated to work ONLY for the highest and purest good of all. This is all that is required, if anything else is requested of the crystal that is inappropriate for any reason, it will not happen. It is possible to programme a crystal to do a specific thing. I always feel that it is important to initially select a crystal with the particular purpose in mind so that you choose a crystal which is happy to be programmed for this.

Many people use crystals which have been programmed to create harmony when placed in a particular room, you may programme a crystal which you keep on your desk to help you focus on work, you may programme a crystal to help to balance and manage your energy field. However, be careful what you ask for and always acknowledge that you should only receive it if it is for your highest good. It is also important that you state clearly what you want, if you ask for a car, it could arrive as a new top of the range model that you cannot afford to run rather than a more modest model which would suit you better. Finally, in order to manifest anything you have to detach from the wish, constantly wanting and wishing for it to appear will not release the request in order for the universe to return it to you. Think of a boomerang and you may get the idea of how these things work!

On the subject of allowing others to share your crystals, this is very much an individual decision. Some people feel a very strong connection to their crystals and do not want other people's energies to affect the vibration that they have connected with, whilst others are happy to share and loan their crystals to others. It is entirely up to the person. On occasions you may feel the need to pass a much loved crystal onto another person, if you are sure that your instincts are correct – do it. It probably means that the crystal has completed it's work with you and needs to move on to another – remember what you give out you get back so let it go willingly.

# Chapter 2

# The Science Bit

### Crystals - A Geological Viewpoint

Crystals can be found within the Earth's crust, upon the surface, in the depths of mines and caves and in the mouths of volcanoes. They are all around us but also (especially when we consider the healing aspect) they are within us for example apatite (a calcium phosphate) is found in bones and teeth.

They grow in all shapes and sizes, shapes and textures and can also be reproduced by man in order to be used in computers, clocks, televisions etc.

We also use crystals to cool our drinks, season our food, paint the walls, relieve headaches, we grow crystals in the "fur" in kettles, even the paper that this book is printed on contains crystals.

Crystals form and live in many varying conditions from the heat of the desert through to the freezing cold of the artic. From inside the Earth to the surrounding solar system.

The earth can be likened to a giant onion which has layers of differing chemical compositions. There is the *Inner Core* which consists of radioactive, solid molten iron and nickel. It is thought to be 3762 - 3958 miles deep and 850 miles wide. Its temperature is 4500C and encompasses 1.7% of the Earth's mass. The next level is the *Outer Core* which is formed of liquid molten minerals, moved by convection and it is this

Outer Core which creates the magnetic field within the earth. It is 793 3762 miles and its temperature is between 2800-3200C. It represents 29.3% of the earths mass. Following this is the *Lower Mantle* which is 652-1793 miles in circumference and the temperature is between 1800-2800C Both the Lower Mantle and the *Upper Mantle,* contain a thick solid shell of hot, rocky silicate minerals. The Upper Mantle covers up to 3 miles beneath sea level and 56 miles beneath continents. It is 249 miles deep and is solid except for a soft, spongy layer which lies next to the crust.

The earth's 'crust' floats on top of molten magma and can be likened to the skin which forms on cooling custard! The ingredients or basic elements within the magma and crust like hydrogen, oxygen, magnesium combine to make minerals which rise to the top of the Earths surface. A simple way of understanding this is to remember a school experiment where we grow crystals by creating a hot solution of water and for example sugar. Whilst the sugar is heated within the water it dissolves and forms a boiling solution. Once the solution has cooled however and is left, it is possible to observe the water evaporating and from the solution single crystal seeds begin to form. As the process continues the sugar will form crystals upon these seeds. Magma is in essence a supersaturated solution of elements which upon cooling, rise to the surface and with different conditions and ingredients form different minerals and crystals. For example when silicon and oxygen combine we get quartz but if water is added to the ingredients we get Opal, with the correct ingredients and conditions Amethyst is formed but if the area is subject to heat radiation then the Amethyst becomes Citrine, conditions between the two form Ametrine. So in order to form Crystals require gases or solutions, the correct temperature, time (usually millions of years) and space (most crystals form within gaps and hollow spaces in the Earth)

# The Structure of the Earth

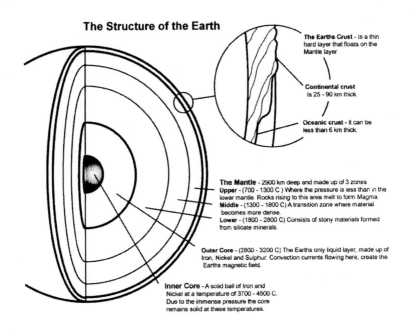

The Earths Crust - Is a thin hard layer that floats on the Mantle layer

Continental crust Is 25 - 90 km thick.

Oceanic crust - It can be less than 6 km thick.

The Mantle - 2900 km deep and made up of 3 zones
Upper - (700 - 1300 C ) Where the pressure is less than in the lower mantle. Rocks rising to this area melt to form Magma.
Middle - (1300 - 1800 C) A transition zone where material becomes more dense.
Lower - (1800 - 2800 C) Consists of stony materials formed from silicate minerals.

Outer Core - (2800 - 3200 C) The Earths only liquid layer, made up of Iron, Nickel and Sulphur. Convection currents flowing here, create the Earths magnetic field.

Inner Core - A solid ball of Iron and Nickel at a temperature of 3700 - 4500 C. Due to the immense pressure the core remains solid at these temperatures.

DIAGRAM 1 Structure of the Earth

There are three categories of rock formation: *Igneous* (directly formed from molten magma below or above ground), It is thought that 90% of the earths surface is igneous. *Sedimentary* (comprising fragments of organic material, weather-beaten rocks which are layered together like stacks of sandwiches and squeezed together, an example of a sedimentary rock would be the Grand Canyon in Arizona, and *Metamorphic* which are rock formations which have been subjected to further pressure and or heat which creates a different inner structure. The Himalyas and Alps are metamorphic rock formations.

Crystallography or the classification of crystals until relatively recently had not changed much since the times of the early Greeks who called these gifts from the earth 'crystallos' which means frozen ice.

Rene Just Hauy, in the late 1700s, discovered after dropping a calcite crystal that the pieces which had shattered on the floor all had retained identical shapes regardless of size. He began to realize that crystals were built up from groups of identically shaped forms which were connected to each other.

Prior to 1912, crystals were analyzed and observed only by the shape that they presented. In 1912 with the advent of the X ray it was possible to look inside the outer structure and it began to be discovered that crystals have a definite repetitive geometric molecular structure. More advances were made in the 1930s when we started to gain a clearer understanding of atoms, electrons and neutrons.

Crystals can be cataloged and identified in a number of varying ways, for example by *colour, texture, transparency, hardness, cleavage* (defined as the way that most minerals break apart and geologist categorise cleavage as perfect, distinct, indistinct or none), *fracture* (again geologist have specific terms to describe how a crystal breaks when it receives a sharp blow, the terms are uneven, conchoidal meaning shell like, hackly meaning jagged and splintery), *chemical constituents* or formula describing a crystals mineral content, a bit like the ingredients which are needed to complete the recipe for a particular formation to occur, *habit* or the way that crystals form (geological terms commonly used to describe this are massive meaning no definite shape, prismatic presenting prisms, dendritic indicating a pattern of growth like a tree, reniform meaning rounded kidney shaped masses, bladed which is indicated by knife blade type shapes presenting within the mineral and botryoidal which looks bubbly not unlike a bunch of grapes) *growth system* and *internal structure*. The following are the most commonly used and well known. Once you become acquainted with these categories it is easy to look up information in relevant geological books and to understand it in order to gain more information on the crystals which you have in your collection.

For a mineral to qualify as a crystal it must have a regular atomic structure. This means that within the crystal there is a consistent reproduction of the intrinsic shape that repeats itself.

Although the ideal crystal would grow in accordance with it's perfect form, due to restrictions placed on it during growth such as space, temperature, chemical composition etc.; it can be rare to encounter a "perfect" specimen.

Although there are thousands of different types of crystals, there are just 7 basic types of pattern:

Trigonal
*Examples of trigonal crystals: Agate, Amethyst, Rose Quartz, Clear Quartz*

Hexagonal
*Examples of hexagonal crystals: Apatite, Beryl, Calcite, Emerald*

Monoclinic
*Examples of monoclinic crystals: Selenite, Actinolite, Moonstone, Kunzite*

Triclinic
*Examples of triclinic crystals: Kyanite, Turquoise, Ulexite (TV Stone)*

Orthorhombic
*Examples of orthorhombic crystals: Staurolite, Prehnite, Peridot,*

Tetragonal
*Examples of tetragonal crystals: Rutile/Rutilated Quartz, Apophyllite*

Cubic
*Examples of cubic crystals: Lodestone, Gold, Lapis Lazuli, Fluorite*

As healers we can be confused when presented with a great selection of gems and minerals. Some of these substances do not have a regular atomic structure and therefore do not qualify as crystals.These materials are known as AMORPHOUS (which means without form). Examples of these, which the healer is likely to come upon, are as follows:

AMBER: This is fossilized tree resin. It has a slightly sticky, plastic feel to it.

OBSIDIAN: A volcanic glass.

LAPIS LAZULI: This is a rock comprised of several minerals eg: Sodalite, Pyrite, Noeslite, Hauyinite and Calcite. This composition is a mixture of the Cubic system and the Trigonal system.

JET: Fossilised coal

MOLDAVITE: An olive green mineral, which is thought to be organic and meteoritic.

TEKTITE: Possibly extra-terrestrial origins.

In addition to the above, the healer may well come into contact with other natural substances such as coral, pearls, metals etc. It is up to each individual's discernment to work with these natural resources in any way that they find their intuition leads them to.

Man made glass, which is marketed, as "Lead Crystal" is amorphous and to all intents and purpose has no healing properties to speak of.

## MOHS Scale

The Mohs Scale is a system created by Friedrich Mohs in 1822 which is still used by Geologists today in order to help catalogue crystals and minerals. It is a way of classifying crystals according to their hardness and the crystal position within the scale relates to how easily the crystal can be scratched, with diamond being the hardest and rated at 10 and Talc being the softest and rated at 1. The Quartz family which include Rose Quartz, Clear Quartz and Amethyst are rated at 7. Minerals which are categorized with a higher number on the scale will scratch those rated at a lower number. Therefore 7 is harder than 6 and 3 is softer than 4.

## Sources of Sedimentary Rocks

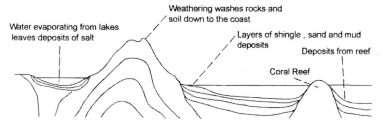

Water evaporating from lakes leaves deposits of salt

Weathering washes rocks and soil down to the coast

Layers of shingle , sand and mud deposits

Deposits from reef

Coral Reef

## Sources of Igneous Rocks

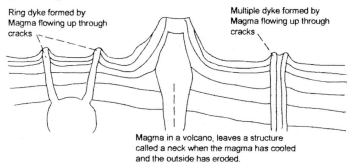

Ring dyke formed by Magma flowing up through cracks

Multiple dyke formed by Magma flowing up through cracks

Magma in a volcano, leaves a structure called a neck when the magma has cooled and the outside has eroded.

## Sources of Metamorphic Rocks

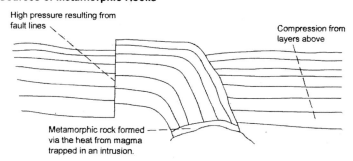

High pressure resulting from fault lines

Compression from layers above

Metamorphic rock formed via the heat from magma trapped in an intrusion.

## How Crystals are formed

DIAGRAM 2 How Crystals Are Formed

## DIAGRAM 4 OF MOHS SCALE OF CRYSTALS

| | | |
|---|---|---|
| 10 | Diamond | the hardest natural substance |
| 9 | Corundum | is easily scratched by Quartz and Topaz |
| 8 | Topaz | can scratch Quartz |
| 7 | Quartz | is hard enough to scratch most surfaces |
| 6 | Feldspar | is still  hard enough to scratch glass |
| 5 | Apatite | can be scratched with a steel point |
| 4 | Fluorite | can be scratched with a penknife blade |
| 3 | Calcite | can be scratched by a coin |
| 2 | Gypsum | will be scratched by a fingernail with difficulty |
| 1 | Talc | easily scratched by a fingernail but can also be scratched by every other mineral as it is the softest mineral of all. |

The hardness rate on the Mohs scale of any crystal is usually found in any good geology book and is something that is worth becoming more aware about as your collection of crystals increase,  because this will provide you with information on care and storage of your crystals. If crystals of different harnesses are stored together the harder crystals in your collection may damage the softer ones.

## Artificial Alteration of Crystals

As well as having the capacity now to grow crystals in laboratory conditions in a very short time as opposed to the millions of years that nature takes, over the centuries man has discovered different methods of altering and "enhancing" gemstones.  This is done for a number of reasons:

i) To improve the existing colour, help maintain it or to produce a colour that does not naturally occur.

ii) To enhance the clarity of the crystal.

iii) To improve the durability of a crystal

Although it is against the law to offer crystals for sale that have been altered in any way without notifying the buyer as well as being unethical, it is unlikely that you will be told before making a purchase. Your supplier may not even be aware of this as crystals generally pass through many hands before finding a home.

The following is a list of treatments that can be applied to different crystals which have an altering effect:

## Chemical Additions and Impregnations
Some crystals such as calcite are coated with a waxy substance which stops flaking and turquoise is often sealed with a plastic resin to make it non porous and to deepen the colour. Sugar is added to agate to make "black onyx" and then blackened by the use of acid.

Other crystals which are either impregnated with or have chemicals added are:

Lapis Lazuli – often stained to enhance colour. Nail varnish remover will reveal if this is the case although some Lapis is waxed as well to prevent this test.

Emeralds are submerged in oil which disguises their imperfections and makes them look generally better, although the appearance can be adversely affected if the oils dry out, it is considered to be standard practice to do this and therefore would not be disclosed at the purchase.

Turquoise – has frequently been crushed and reconstituted with resin to make it more stable and solid, it is sometimes immersed in oil or coloured to further improve its appearance. Generally Howlite which is white is dyed a deep turquoise colour and passed off as turquoise.

## Heat Treatment

This is used to improve the colour of many gemstones such as aquamarine, tourmaline, rubies and sapphires whilst heat treatment can also alter colours of sapphire, topaz, zircon, amethyst for example turns to citrine when heated. It is also sometimes used to improve the clarity of gems such as sapphires and rubies. In areas of naturally high earth temperature such as those where volcanic activity happens this process will occur naturally and it can be difficult to distinguish the naturally occurring effects from the artificially created. Again it is considered to be standard practice to heat treat sapphires and rubies and again is not disclosed to the buyer upon purchase. Possible crystals which can be affected by heat treatment are:

Amethyst – if heated can turn to citrine but if specifically heated to 500c may turn green and is known as prasiolite

Clear Quartz - can be heated to create man made smoky or black quartz which is also naturally occurring.

Tigers Eye – when heated can turn from yellow to red, brown or blue.

## Irradiation

Irradiation can be used to produce a variety of shades and colours. It is commonly used with clear topaz which turns it various shades of blue and diamonds which can alter the colour somewhat. Whilst the heat treatment is generally permanent, irradiation can be unstable and it is possible to reverse the process by heating. Crystals which may have been irradiated include:

Citrine
Smoky Quartz

Apart from their therapeutic properties, crystals contain a form of electricity known as piezoelectricity. This energy is emitted when a crystal is exposed to pressure causing an electric polarization equivalent to the pressure which has been applied. This can be shown as a voltage and the following is a list of the uses that we put this charge to in everyday life:

Tourmaline is used in starter motors in cars

We use diamonds in record player arms to transmit the sounds

We use crystals in LCD or Liquid Crystal Displays for clocks, calculators, wristwatches, thermometers and television screens. They are efficient to use as the level of power consumption is low but they provide very clear displays

As well as LCD, solid quartz or occasionally ruby are used in the mechanism in older watches and clocks. Crystals are used in the solar panels which store the sun's energy in order to generate electricity

Because of their ability to polarize light in a specific way crystals are used also as optical lenses, in optic fibres, Light Emitting Diodes, more commonly known as LEDs are considered to be the light source of the future and these use crystal semi-conductors. Crystal radiation detector are also available to find and measure the presence of all types of radiation.

The most easily accessible but also the most common family within the crystal realms is the Quartz Family. It has been said that the Earth is made up of 70% Quartz which can be found all over the world.

Include within the Quartz family are the  sand grains found on some beaches. These grains have been washed down from mountains by rivers and streams. When the  sea's waves ebb and flow the grains of sand are rounded a little more by the motion and movement of the water.

Quartz crystals are usually six-sided with a point at one end and although quartz can be seen in many different colours and shapes, all quartz have an identical chemical structure which is silicon dioxide. This is a combination of silicon and oxygen. Quartz sometimes forms in Geodes which are also known as "Thunder Eggs" or "Potato Stones" . These are created around gas bubbles within a mixture of volcanic lava and magma and when opened, you find a mini cave of quartz crystals which grow towards the center.

The following is a list of crystals belonging to the Quartz family:

Agate ~ can be found in a variety of colours but is also frequently dyed with quite garish colours
Amethyst ~ Varying shades of purple
Aventurine ~ iridescent green due to Mica, less commonly gold brown
Basinite ~ Black
Blue Quartz ~ Dull blue
Carnelian ~ Varying shades of orange
Carnelian-Onyx ~ red with a white upper layer
Chalcedony ~ strong bluey grey
Citrine ~ pale yellow to strong yellow through to brown, this can be man made by radiating a piece of Amethyst
Crysoprase ~ strong apple green

Dendritic Agate ~ translucent with featherlike markings, grey white

Flint ~ black , grey and white primarily which can be opaque and flat

Fossilized Wood ~ Brown, grey or red

Hawk's Eye ~ grey/blue or blue/green

Heliotrope, Bloodstone ~ dark green sometimes has red markings

Jasper ~ all colours sometimes has markings such as stripes or spots

Moss Agate ~ clear or opaque with dark green inclusions which almost look like encased moss

Onyx ~ black, sometimes has a layer of white

Opal ~ transclucent or opalescent comes in a milky base shot through with multi colours, also less common to have red or yellow fire opal

Prase ~ light green

Prasiolite ~ light green

Quartz Cat's Eye ~ grey, green, yellow, brown, white

Rock Crystal ~ Colourless or white

Rose Quartz ~ pale pink through to a violet pink

Sard ~ red brown

Sard-Onyx ~ brown with a white upper layer

Smoky Quartz ~ clear quartz which has a smoky brown or black tinge to it

Star Quartz ~ ordinary clear quartz which when polished have a star shaped inclusion

Tigers Eye ~ Iridescent comes in gold/yellow, red, blue, brown

When working with Quartz crystals and in particular, clear quartz crystals it is possible to find them in a number of manifestations. As I have mentioned above, they can be found in Geode form. The following are the most common types of formation:

**Single Pointed or Termination Clear Quartz:** The crystal is usually six-sided and forms a pyramid at the point. Sometimes the crystal is cloudy and some healers believe that a clear crystal has a masculine quality to it's energy whilst a cloudy crystal has a more feminine quality. Has a very directional energy flow and is excellent for clearing blocks and energizing.

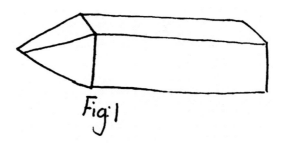

Fig. 1

**Double Pointed or Termination Clear Quartz:** Much less common than the single termination and therefore much more expensive, the double terminated crystal has a point at both ends. They are considered by most healers to be self contained as the energy flows in two directions (a bit like a figure of 8). Thought to be ideal for meditation and programming as well as placing on the body to carry out a general re-balancing of the energy field.

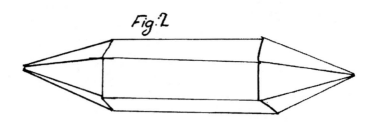

Fig. 2

**Cluster:** A group of points which share a common base. The energy within the cluster is not so directional which makes them ideal for placing in a room. They are also good for providing a "bed" to energise tired crystals.

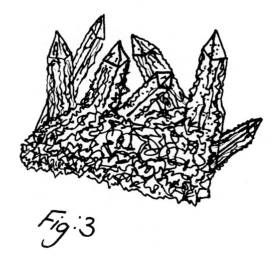

Fig.3

**Rock Crystal:** Energetically, a more diffuse, gentle energy. This crystal is commonly faceted and shaped by man into geometric shapes which will add a focus to the energy.

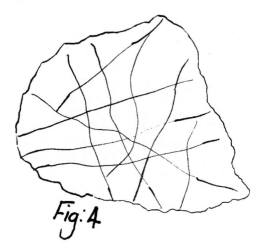

Fig.4

**Phantom Crystal:** Sometimes known as "ghost" crystals, this crystal has a mineral inclusion which is caused by a brief change in conditions at some point during the crystal's growth which results in a thin coating of another mineral over the surface of the crystal. The crystal then continues it growth in the normal way, trapping the mineral outline of it's previous self. Water can

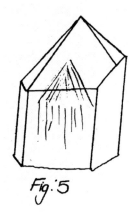

Fig. 5

also be trapped in a similar way (known as enhydro crystals) and crystals can also have internal fractures which cause a coloured rainbow effect to appear within the crystal.

**Elestial Quartz** – This crystal can help to activate the Akashic Records or previous knowledge from past lives. They are sometimes known as "Cathedral Crystals" and have a number of upwardly pointing crystal terminations which have merged together. Often forms in smoky quartz.

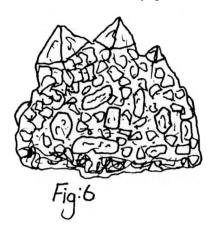

Fig:6

28

**Laser crystals** – Slender and thin these crystal formations taper to a fine point – some healers see these crystals as spiritual scalpels

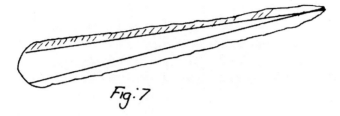

*Fig. 7*

**Record Keeper** – These crystals have perfect raised triangles on one of the crystal sides – seen as containing information from the Akashic records

*Fig. 8*

**Self Healing Crystals** – On the crystal where it has broken, usually around the base, a number of small crystals have formed. Obviously seen as a tool to aid the healing processes within us.

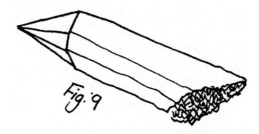

Fig. 9

**Sceptre** – single, naturally formed crystal with a termination which protrudes through a large base – believed by some to have been used extensively in Atlantis by high priests and priestesses as symbols of power, they can be used to invoke power and knowledge from that time.

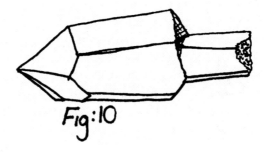

Fig: 10

**Singing Crystals** – These crystals emit a clear note when gently touched together, generally smaller than laser crystals but similar in appearance. They can be used to activate and translate knowledge from other dimensions.

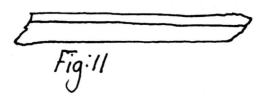

Fig:11

**Twinned or Tantric Crystals** – Sharing a single base, two or more single terminations have formed and grown together. A crystal is considered to be a twin when the growth is uniform and they lie side by side – its uses would be to promote a loving and balanced relationship, this may be with another person or with your Higher Self. A Tantric crystal is where crystals share a single base but the growth of the crystals may not be uniform and there may be some terminations which are more dominant than others even though they are parallel, the qualities of a Tantric crystal would lend itself to enhancing teamwork and group co-operation

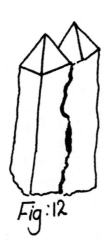

Fig:12

**Window Crystals** – At the tip of the crystal a large diamond shaped facet forms an extra face. Used to aid clairvoyance and inner knowledge.

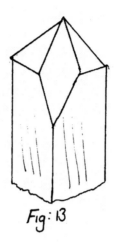

*Fig: 13*

## Colour

As Crystal Healers it is important that we are aware of the ability of colour to affect the energy field because, when we use crystals, we are indeed working with the energetic effects of the crystals colour. Usually, when selecting a crystal to work with, one of the first things that draw us to a crystal is its colour and colour is the first thing we take into account when trying to identify a crystal. The true colour of a crystal can be ascertained by scratching a crystal on an unglazed surface. This will leave something geologists call a streak and this residue of dust is an indication of the crystals proper colour.

The colour of a crystal is brought about by three different factors:

1. The chemical composition of the stone and in some cases the "impurity" of the chemical composition. For example, Aventurine displays a shimmering silvery green sheen, which are as a result of the fuchsite mica flakes, which make up its composition.

2. Defects in the crystal lattice which affect the way that the light passes through the crystal, modifying it either by reflection, refraction and diffraction (see diagram)

3. Interference of light. In other words, the way that the crystal interacts with light. When a stone absorbs all light frequencies it will appear black, conversely a white stone reflects the entire colour spectrum and doesn't absorb any light. Opaque or translucent crystals absorb light rays, which are slowed and bent or diffused (refracted or diffracted) according to the atomic arrangement within the crystals.

Lustre is a word used to describe the effects of daylight as it is reflected from a mineral's surface. The different types of lustre can be classified as follows: *pearly, waxy, iridescent* (shimmering, possibly with rainbow colours), *chatoyancy* (shiny silky appearance which shimmers), *adamantine* (diamond like sparkle), *earthy* (non reflective, dull), *silky* (a sheen like effect created by a mass of very small hair like crystals), *greasy* (may feel slippery or oily and appear to be wet), *resinous* (looks a little dull, like plastic), *vitreous* (looks like the porcelain which we make sinks and baths from), *metallic* (shiny and reflective)

Depending on how the atomic structure affects the light photons determines the colour of the crystal. The slower frequencies appear red/orange, the faster frequencies appear blue/violet whilst the medium frequencies appear yellow/green.

| Colour | Complementary Colour | Wavelength of colour nm |
|--------|---------------------|------------------------|
| Violet | Green/Yellow | 400-424 |
| Blue | Yellow | 424-491 |
| Green | Red | 491-570 |
| Yellow | Blue | 570-585 |
| Orange | Green/Blue | 585-647 |
| Red | Green | 647-700 |

Therefore a crystal, which appears to be red will, in fact, be absorbing green light and vice versa.

Refraction can be illustrated by passing a laser beam through a transparent substance such as a crystal. The light enters the substance and slows down. It bends as it passes from air to substance. The light speeds up again as it pass through the substance but the process has caused the light to bend or refract.

When light is traveling into Earth from the sun or stars, it passes through air at about 300,000 km per second and slows to 193,000 when passing through Quartz or 124,000 km per second through diamond. With each crystal type the speed at which light is processed varies.

So crystals, due to the differing chemical compositions, formations etc., are able to filter certain parts of the spectrum and thereby release or hold on to certain colours. We can begin to see that Colour Healers could possibly regard crystals as "batteries" holding specific colour energies.

Many geologist use different descriptions to indicate the way that light passes through a crystal. When light does not pass through a crystal it is described as *opaque*, if light does not clearly reflect through the crystal even though it is passing through it, it is described as *translucent*. When you can see through a crystal it is described as *transparent.*

Light comprises of a combination of colours which when mixed appear white. The light is made up from varying wavelengths of energy which appear to us as different colours:

> Red
> Orange
> Yellow
> Green
> Blue
> Indigo
> Violet

In his book, *"The Colour Therapy Workbook"*, Theo Gimbal defines Colour Healing thus:

"Colour Therapy harness the energies of light and the colours of the spectrum to help a wide variety of health problems and to allow us to harmonize with our natural rhythms and energies, and generally to become more balanced. It does this by locating and then correcting colour imbalances in the aura, the energy field surrounding the body"

Through this description we can see that the colours ascribed to the energy centres of the body (Chakras) relate to a method of healing that can be utilised to correct energetic imbalances. Listed below are colours and their definitions and possible suggested theraputic uses:

## RED:
**Meaning:** Strength, energy, vitality, life, sexuality, warning, power, alertness, contraction, heat, danger, blood.
**Therapeutic use:** Low blood pressure, lack of energy, impotence, inactivity, and drowsiness, lack of interest or zest for life, initiate and empower ideas, creat a positive impact.

## ORANGE:
**Meaning:** Happiness, dance, joy, independence, carelessness, creativity.
**Therapeutic use:** Anti-depressant, energy also for low blood pressure when red is too powerful, release, stimulates creativity, antidote to shock.

## YELLOW:
**Meaning:** Detachment, intellect, thinking, judgmental, criticism, concentration.
**Therapeutic Use:** Rheumatism, arthritis, skeletal conditions, alleviate confusion, fear and anxiety, strenthen immune system.

## GREEN:
**Meaning:** Harmony, balance, stability and neutrality, equilibrium, freedom.
**Therapeutic Use:** Cleansing, purifying, cancer, balancing emotions, new ideas.

## TURQUOISE:
**Meaning:** Purity, immunity, calmness, protection, confidence and strength.
**Therapeutic Use:** Anti-inflammatory, AIDS (HIV), nervous tension, enhance personal energy and inner confidence.

## BLUE:
**Meaning:** Relaxation, sleep, peace, expansion, communication, detachment and relaxation.
**Therapeutic Use:** High blood pressure, stress, asthma, migraine, calming, aids self-reflection.

**VIOLET:**
**Meaning:** Dignity, divinity, honour, value, hope, balance and integration.
**Therapeutic use:** Hopelessness, lack of self-respect, loss of self-appreciation, building personality, calm hyperactivity, aids natural healing process.

**MAGENTA:**
**Meaning:** Selflessness, meditation, perfection, release, let go.
**Therapeutic use:** Changes, freedom, to let go of old habits no longer applicable. The final transition into spirit at the correct time.

**WHITE:**
**Meaning:** Innocence, untouched, isolation, wisdom, fresh start and clarity.
**Therapeutic use:** Total neutrality, absolute clarity and truth.

**BLACK:**
**Meaning:** The unfathomable depth, holding all colours, which are earthbound, experience.
**Therapeutic use:** Aids self-control, maintains persoanl space, provides inconspicuosness.

**GREY:**
**Meaning:** Service, dedication, neutrality, efficiency
**Therapeutic use:** Enhances ability to stabilize and think things through more clearly.

**BROWN:**
**Meaning:** Sacrifice, dedication, commitment, warmth, stability.
**Therapeutic use:** Aids with detachment, can be a supporting colour.

# Sacred Geometry

As we have mentioned above, crystals have an internal geometric shape or structure, which the naked eye cannot see. However this pattern links with the shapes that we create when placing crystals on or around the body to form varying geometric shapes or grids which also affect the therapeutic processes occurring during a crystal healing session. This works on both a macrocosmic (what you can see i.e. the way the crystals are placed) and a microcosmic (what you cant see i.e. the internal structure of the crystals used) levels which means that there is many levels of consciousness being affected during the course of the treatment.

There is a growing awakening (or should it be reawakening?) awareness of the power of differing shapes which appears to be knowledge that our ancestors knew of, particularly architects and artists for example, and worked with which until recently has now been buried deep within the mists of time.

In a further chapter we will work with combining crystals and specific shapes to form grids for healing.

A final point to be made as the awareness of crystal therapy grows is that we are using a resource that has been taken from the earth. This resource is not sustainable. It takes millions of years for a crystal to grow and as crystal therapy grows in popularity, it is only a matter of time before the demand outstrips the earths ability to supply.

In ancient times crystals were taken as they became exposed this is known as surface mining. Nowadays crystals are mined sometimes by placing explosives in the earth or by sandblasting, following this some crystals are placed in acid to clean them. In addition to this enforced child labour under the

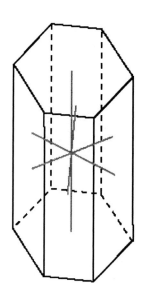

## Hexagonal System
Examples of Hexagonal Crystals :-
Apatite,
Beryl,
Calcite

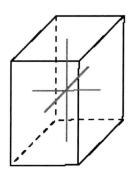

## Tetragonal System
Examples of Tetragonal Crystals :-
Quartz,
Apophyllite

DIAGRAM 4a Crystal systems

**39**

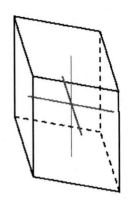

## Triclinic Crystal System
Examples of Triclinic Crystals :-
Kyanite,
Turquoise,
Ulexite

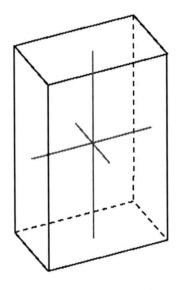

## Monoclinic Crystal System
Examples of Monoclinic Crystals :-
Actinolite,
Moonstone,
Kunzite

DIAGRAM 4b Crystal systems

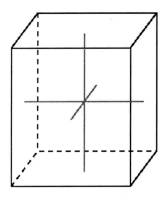

## Orthorhombic Crystal System
Examples of Othorhombic Crystals :-
Staurolite,
Prehnite,
Peridot

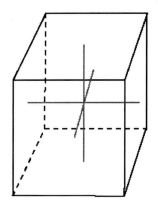

## Cubic Crystal System
Examples of Cubic Crystals :-
Lodestone,
Gold,
Lapis,
Lazuli,
Fluorite

DIAGRAM 4c Crystal systems

most appalling conditions for very low rates of pay are common practice in the poorer mining areas such as India and Brazil for example. It is important therefore to acquire crystals only when we are truly drawn to them and not to simply buy them without due thought and consideration.

You may wish to use the following Attunement Sheet in order to keep a record of information on crystals, which are in your collection:

# INDIVIDUAL CRYSTAL INFORMATION SHEET

Crystals Name:                          Family Group Name:


Crystal System:                         Chemical Composition:


Countries of origin:                    Hardness:


Crystal Formation:

Colours:

Other Significant Information - **Special care, poisonous, contra-indications:**



Your interpretation of the significance and uses of this crystal

# Chapter 3

# The Quartz Family of Crystals

Although there are thousands of crystals, there are only 7 crystal 'families' or groups of crystal. The most easily accessible but also the most common family within the crystal realms is the Quartz Family. It has been said that the Earth is made up of 70% Quartz which can be found all over the world.

Included within the Quartz family are the sand grains found on some beaches. These grains have been washed down from mountains by rivers and streams. When the seas waves ebb and flow the motion and movement of the water round the grains of sand a little more.

Quartz crystals are usually six-sided with a point at one end and although quartz can be seen in many different colours and shapes, all quartz has an identical chemical structure, which is silicon dioxide. This is a combination of silicon and oxygen. Quartz sometimes forms in Geodes, which are also known as 'Thunder Eggs' or 'Potato Stones'. These are created around gas bubbles within a mixture of volcanic lava and magma and when opened, you find a mini cave of quartz crystals, which grow, towards the center.

The following is a list of crystals belonging to the Quartz family:

**Agate** ~ can be found in a variety of colours but is also frequently dyed with quite garish colours

**Amethyst** ~ Varying shades of purple

**Aventurine** ~ iridescent green due to Mica, less commonly gold brown

**Basinite** ~ Black

**Blue Quartz** ~ Dull blue

**Carnelian** ~ Varying shades of orange

**Carnelian-Onyx** ~ red with a white upper layer

**Chalcedony** ~ strong bluey grey

**Citrine** ~ pale yellow to strong yellow through to brown, this can be man made by radiating a piece of Amethyst

**Crysoprase** ~ strong apple green

**Dendritic Agate** ~ translucent with featherlike markings, grey white

**Flint** ~ black, grey and white primarily which can be opaque and flat

**Fossilized Wood** ~ Brown, grey or red

**Hawks Eye** ~ grey/blue or blue/green

**Heliotrope, Bloodstone** ~ dark green sometimes has red markings

**Jasper** ~ all colours sometimes has markings such as stripes or spots

**Moss Agate** ~ clear or opaque with dark green inclusions which almost look like encased moss

**Onyx** ~ black, sometimes has a layer of white

**Opal** ~ translucent or opalescent comes in a milky base shot through with multi colours, also less common to have red or yellow fire opal

**Prase** ~ light green

**Prasiolite** ~ light green

**Quartz Cats Eye** ~ grey, green, yellow, brown, white

**Rock Crystal** ~ Colourless or white

**Rose Quartz** ~ pale pink through to a violet pink

**Sard** ~ red brown

**Sard-Onyx** ~ brown with a white upper layer

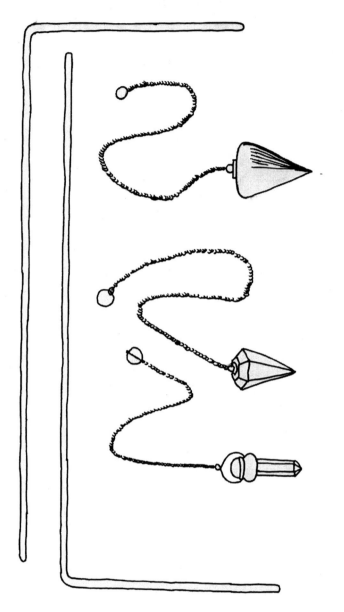

DIAGRAM 6 - Pendulums

**Smoky Quartz** ~ clear quartz which has a smoky brown or black tinge to it
**Star Quartz** ~ ordinary clear quartz which when polished have a star shaped inclusion
**Tigers Eye** ~ Iridescent comes in gold/yellow, red, blue, brown

When working with Quartz crystals and in particular, clear quartz crystals it is possible to find them in a number of manifestations. As I have mentioned above, they can be found in Geode form. The following are the most common types of formation:

**Single Pointed or Termination Clear Quartz**: The crystal is usually six-sided and forms a pyramid at the point. Sometimes the crystal is cloudy and some healers believe that a clear crystal has a masculine quality to its energy whilst a cloudy crystal has a more feminine quality. Has a very directional energy flow and is excellent for clearing blocks and energizing.

**Double Pointed or Termination Clear Quartz**: Much less common than the single termination and therefore much more expensive, the double terminated crystal has a point at both ends. They are considered by most healers to be self-contained as the energy flows in two directions (a bit like a figure of 8). Thought to be ideal for meditation and programming as well as placing on the body to carry out a general re-balancing of the energy field.

**Cluster:** A group of points, which share a common base. The energy within the cluster is not so directional which makes them ideal for placing in a room. They are also good for providing a bed to energise tired crystals.

**Rock Crystal:** Energetically, a more diffuse, gentle energy. This crystal is commonly faceted and shaped by man into geometric shapes, which will add a focus to the energy.

**Phantom Crystal:** Sometimes known as ghost crystals, this crystal has a mineral inclusion which is caused by a brief change in conditions at some point during the crystals growth which results in a thin coating of another mineral over the surface of the crystal. The crystal then continues its growth in the normal way, trapping the mineral outline of its previous self. Water can also be trapped in a similar way and crystals can also have internal fractures, which cause a coloured rainbow effect to appear within the crystal.

**Lead Crystal:** Sometimes mistaken for quartz crystal, commonly found in chandeliers but more recently in the feng shui shapes which are hung from windows to divert chi energy and reflect rainbows into a room as the sun passes through them. These are man-made.

# Chapter 4

# Subtle Energy Systems of The Body

## 1. Dowsing

Dowsing is an extremely effective way to assess the health and energetic flow of subtle energy systems around the body whether this is for chakras, subtle bodies or meridians.

Anyone can learn to dowse. All that is required is an open mind and a pendulum or simply a piece of cotton with a ring threaded through it. (Some dowsers use rods but these are not really convenient when working on the body as they are too unwieldy).

A good way to start to dowse is to hold a pendulum over a cleansed crystal. Ensure that you are relaxed and comfortable, simply ask either mentally or verbally for the energy of the crystal to connect to the pendulum and indicate a positive energy flow. When this happens, it invariably will indicate a positive response. Once this has been achieved, ask questions with yes answers and the pendulum should respond. When you are confident of your positive response, ask questions to which you expect a 'no' answer. The response may not be in what you would expect to be the logical route. It may not go in the opposite direction to your 'yes'.

Some people discover through the course of working with a pendulum that they have no movement may indicate a

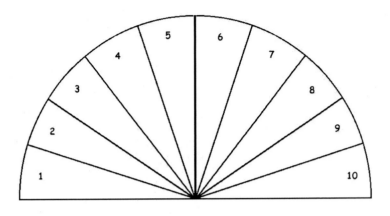

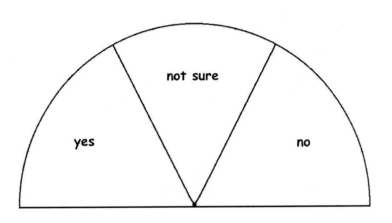

DIAGRAM 7 Yes/No/Neutral & Numbers

neutral swing for others, neutral at all. Alternatively, you could practice with these charts:

Take time to work with the techniques until you feel assured that you are happy with the responses you are getting. As you grow in confidence, you will find that you will be able to detect not only positive or negative responses but also be shown the flow of energy and from this you can discover whether the energy flow is over energized, under energized or just right. In order to work as efficiently as possible it is important to make sure that you ask the pendulum for answers to relevant questions and that they are posed in such a way as for the response to be given as a yes or no if you have a neutral then it would be possible for a maybe!

! So when you want to find the energy levels of the chakras for example, you should ask the question "Please show me the energy level of each chakra as I dowse it" rather than "Show me the Crown Chakra". With the first question the pendulum will show you varying degrees of spin depending on the energy flow through the chakra, with the second question you will merely be shown where the particular chakra is sited.

Other useful questions to bear in mind would be "Has the answer not yet been decided?", "Do I have permission to know the answer to this question at this time?" and "Is there anything I can do to influence the result?" When dowsing for negative energy whether it is from another person or earth energies always ensure that you are fully protected.

As with crystals many people prefer to keep their pendulums for their own use only. Always ask someone if you want to borrow their pendulum.

A word of warning only dowse when you are in a neutral state of mind. When dowsing you are getting in touch with your intuitive consciousness and if the logical mind becomes involved the results will go haywire. You should also never dowse for another person without their agreement.

In addition to dowsing many people can sense subtle energy. It is possible to become sensitive to the flow. A good technique to learn how it feels is to rub both hands together and then draw them apart, about the distance that they would be if a balloon were in between them. Then with the eyes closed, gently try to 'bounce' the hands together. Some people sense and resist, not unlike 2 magnets repelling each other, some people sense heat, tingling or coolness, sometimes described as a slight breeze. If you can feel this, try to run your hands over the chakra centers, holding the arms outstretched on either side of the person. As you scan the body, you will feel similar sensations and the person you are scanning may well be aware of your connecting with them through a feeling of pressure, heat, coolness etc at these points.

If you intend to use crystals in a therapeutic way, it is important that you learn how to monitor the effects that they have on the energy systems within the body.

## Historical Overview of Chakras

The existence of Chakras have been recognized, accepted and utilized by many diverse cultures and religions, separated through time and geography.

Chakra is a Sanskrit word used by Hindus meaning 'wheel of light' but religions such as Judaism, Islam, Hinduism, Buddhism and even early Christianity have worked with these energy centers and incorporated them into rituals and understandings. It is interesting to note that a possible reason why someone is drawn to a particular religion in a lifetime may be to focus on a specific Chakra energy in depth. It is suggested by Rosalyn L Bruyere in her book entitled "*Wheels*

*Of Light"* that many religions are focused more on one center of consciousness rather than encompassing all of them equally. She argues that Judaism places an emphasis on the 3rd Chakra, which is intellectually based, whilst Islam focuses more on the 6th Chakra working as it does with specific prayer postures relating to the forehead. Christianity is more heart centered with its emphasis on unconditional love and forgiveness.

This is not to say that any one religion is superior or inferior to another merely that people drawn to certain religions find that they can work with a Chakra center on a more intense basis.

In the West, the early British Theosophists who formed part of Alice Bailey's group during Victorian times visited India and returned with a basic understanding of Chakras gleaned from these travels. They initiated a resurgence of interest and understanding of Chakras which continues today within the western world, fuelled by our increased ability to travel and read about other cultures and beliefs.

Chakras are intersections within the body which link with the Meridian systems and carry prana, chi or life force energy throughout the body.

A way of visualizing them is to see the Chakras as roundabouts and the energy lines or meridians as motorways, with accupressure points as mini roundabouts which flow in and out of the Chakras.

Although we have 7 major Chakras - see diagram - there are many more minor Chakras which are contained in the body such as in the palms of the hands, soles of the feet, tips of the fingers and so on.

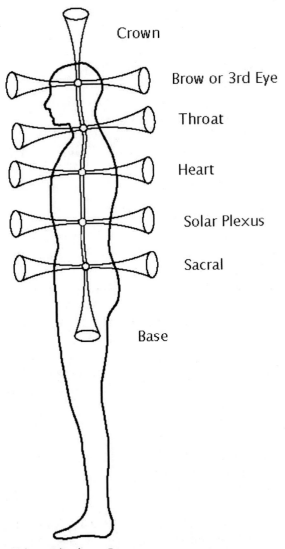

Crown

Brow or 3rd Eye

Throat

Heart

Solar Plexus

Sacral

Base

The Chakra System

CHAKRA DIAGRAM 8 Basic Chakra system and diagram of individual Chakra and how the energy flows.

Chakras are described by clairvoyants who have the ability to see the energy field of the body as spinning wheels or vortexes of energy. The seven major Chakras spin in alternate, opposite directions, taking in life-force energy and releasing processed energy at the same time. The action of the chakras on the life force energy is to act as transmuters by transforming the energy into the physiological and hormonal systems of the body which in turn affect cellular changes on a physical level.

Many healers consider that the front of the chakra relates to the individual's feelings and the back of the chakra relates to the will of the person. The chakras sited at the head, brow and throat are considered to be the "higher" chakras with the heart chakra acting as link to the lower three – solar plexus, sacral and base symbolizing a link between heaven and earth.

On a healthy person, these energy centers would be reasonably well balanced and aligned. Where there is an imbalance or misalignment, there may well eventually be a physical manifestation of this as an illness. These imbalances can be brought about by shock or trauma but also from underlying issues, which are not dealt with such as stress or a dysfunctional relationship, for example, whether they affect us on a mental or emotional or even spiritual level. The way that we treat our body through diet or substance abuse for example will also have a direct effect on these centers. For this reason healers tend to focus a great deal on providing the necessary energy whether this be through providing Spiritual Healing (sometimes known as Faith Healing), Reiki, Colour Therapy, Gem and Flower Essence Therapy, Crystal Therapy, of course, or some of the more conventional therapies such as Acupuncture or Homeopathy in order to bring about an energetic rebalance. These are all forms of what is termed vibrational healing and Chakras respond better to these types of treatment generally than to any other form of healing.

It is important to note that these centers can be over-energized as well as under-energized. For the majority of healers who do not have the benefit from the form of clairvoyance where they can actually see the Chakras and any imbalances, it is possible to use methods such as dowsing, muscle testing, intuition, or simply feeling the energy flow in order to determine where to direct healing energy.

Each Chakra has a relation to physical aspects of the body, but it can also be linked to emotional and mental traits as well. There are colour correspondences which relate to each Chakra as well and can be useful as they can help us when we attempt to rebalance and align them.

Below is a basic list of Chakra correspondences:

### Base Chakra
Sometimes known as the Root Chakra or Muladhara. This is situated at the base of the spine and promotes the basic physical survival instinct. It is connected to materialism, courage, and vitality and links us to the earth. Its traditional colour is red and it relates to the physical organs

### Sacral Chakra
Alternative names for this center are Svadhisthana or navel. It is situated approximately 2 inches below the navel. Its role is to generate sexual energies, creativity, initiate new ideas and promote endurance, vitality and strength. The traditional colour is Orange and it relates to the physical organs

### Solar Plexus Chakra
Or Manipura is found just above the bellybutton, below the rib cage. It is connected with personal power, personality and the ego, as well as being the energetic mouth of the body where life force energy is taken in. The traditional colour is seen as Yellow and on the physical level it relates to the Solar Plexus area and large intestine.

**Heart Chakra**
This center, known as Anahata, can be found in the center of the chest at the level of the heart. It relates to emotions such as compassion and love ultimately to the promotion of unconditional love of the self and others. It is linked physically with the physical heart, thymus, circulatory system, cellular structure and all the other muscles which work automatically without any need for conscious thought on our part. There are two colours which are thought to relate to this center, pink and green.

**Throat Chakra**
Sanskrit name for this center is Visuddha, it is situated at the base of the neck where it meets the clavicle and sternum. It is related to all aspects of communication. It is important to note that although this relates to making oneself understood by others it also relates to us understanding others when they communicate with us. It also is linked to creativity whether that may be from the written word, painting through to talking. Physically, it can be linked with the thyroid, neck and shoulders and the jaw. Associated colour with this Chakra is Light Blue.

**The Brow or 3rd Eye Chakra**
It has the Sanskrit name of Ajna, and is placed in between the level where the eyebrows meet. It is a center that is linked with clairvoyant and intuitive abilities and many people seek to develop this center in order to achieve greater levels of psychic ability such as clairvoyance, telepathy etc. Physically it relates to the cerebellum, nose, central nervous system, the pituitary glands and the left eye. The pineal and pituitary glands combine together to help activate this center. Colour associations are Indigo.

**Crown Centre**
Known in Sanskrit as Sahasrara, this is the final major center. Its focus is thought to be our spiritual connection with

Effects of poor diet on the body

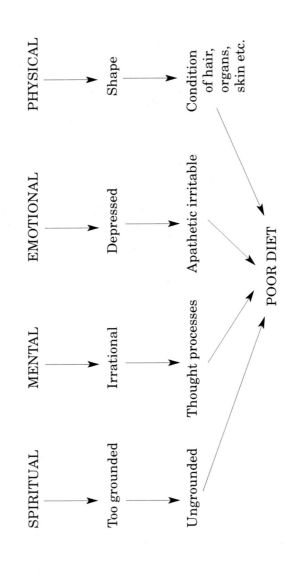

DIAGRAM 9  Effects of poor diet on the body

God, the cosmos or universe. It empowers enlightenment, dynamic thought and spirituality. Physically it is linked with the cerebrum, the right eye and the pineal gland. Colours related to this center are purple, white and sometimes gold.

Chakras may be out of balance for any number of reasons. In order to treat a person effectively it may be necessary to identify possible reasons for the imbalances, which the patient can address in order for the healing to be more effective. It is also extremely important that the healer makes the patient aware that he or she should also consider the mainstream treatment available, as Crystal Therapy is a COMPLEMENTARY therapy rather than an ALTERNATIVE therapy.

Bad diet, troubled relationships, stress, invasive treatments for ailments, drug and alcohol abuse, inappropriate spiritual connections - these are just a few of the life experiences open to all of us which can cause the chakras to become out of balance and alignment. This in turn can lead to disease of the system, which ultimately can manifest in the physical as illness or disease. Mainstream medicine is now beginning to accept that cancer can sometimes be traced back to a trauma 2-3 years previously. As we have already established, the physical effects of stress upon the body are well documented from increased blood pressure to nervous skin disorders and so on. If you are to aid the patient to reach a point of balance and alignment there may be lifestyle changes which the patient needs to consider in addition to the healing offered.

It is important for everybody to take responsibility for their own healing. The chart above shows how something as basic as poor diet can affect us and create imbalances within our energetic system.

# Possible Symptons of Chakra Dysfunction

### Base Chakra
Feels unworthy, not understood, not loved too materialistic. Wants more because of lack of security. Dominant, intense survival instinct (maybe not looked after as a child), maybe an experience from this lifetime or others. Doesn't want to be "here". Problems with legs, hips, coccyx

### Sacral Chakra
Great difficulty in trusting, fear of being left alone but fear of loving. Imbalances in sexual contact i.e. frigid or promiscuous, sexual dependency. Fear of having a relationship, wanting it too much, tendency to be tense about sexuality, instability, addictions to drugs - abuse or misuse can also be addicted to anything even love. Problems with large intestine.

### Solar Plexus
Power centre. Helpless and weak. Allows themselves to be controlled or are controlled. Lose natural ability to balance controlling and dominating. Shows off, struggles for success. Can hold suppressed anger and possibly suddenly expresses this through anger or rage. Misuse of power, aggressive, enjoying arguments. Passive power through helplessness. Digestive problems, migraine, immune system difficulties.

### Heart Chakra
Loneliness, lost, not enough attention, sad without a reason. Guilt. Possible origins not enough love when we are little. Tendency to exaggerate or to set aside own desires of others. Role of victim. Constant search for new relationships. Depressed, repressed, fear of being own self. Asthma, air based allergies such as Hay Fever for example

## Throat Chakra

Unable to express themselves, talking, singing, movement. Critical, possibly punished in this or other lives for speaking their own truth. Could possibly have been spiritual teachers in past lives. Feelings of not being good enough, not being understood. Can be blocked with unexpressed grief. Men can be more susceptible to blockages in this area due to finding it difficult to express their emotions in our society. Tendency to manipulate or lie. Lack of clarity, unable to make up their minds about things - this can also manifest in the Solar Plexus. Thyroid difficulties, neck problems.

## Brow Chakra

Very critical, very judgmental. Not happy or convinced, nothing is good enough. Great difficulty in coping when intuition and logic struggle with each other. Unable to see links or patterns in things, not wanting to look beyond the obvious.

## Crown Chakra

Disturbed connection with the Divine and or universal energy. Rarely 'blocked' but often out of balance. Can manifest as delusion, illusion, only interested in "spiritual" stuff or "worldly" stuff - can't cope with both. Dyslexia, dyspraxia, general co-ordination.

Base and Heart work as a pair, Throat and Sacral, Solar Plexus and Crown. Sometimes it is the balance between the pair that is the problem i.e. dominance.

# Cleaʀíng

In order to clear these blocks/imbalance, it is important to:

1. Understand why WE have allowed them to be created in the first place.

2. Not to project guilt and blame onto others.

3. Try to see what it has taught us.

4. Ask, "Have I learned my lesson?"

5. Forgive - especially yourself as well as others.


Try to become conscious of negative thoughts and emotions. Know that it is possible to release them through understanding of the greater truth. Try to work from a position of unconditional love and compassion for ourselves and others.

It is possible to use visualization to great effect when working with the chakras. All that is required is a little time and quiet space where you can sit comfortably for a few moments and be assured of no interruption. Then close your eyes, and take your focus to the Crown Chakra either visualize an energy link to the Universe flowing into the top of the crown or, if you prefer, try to visualize the appropriate colour, in this case purple or white perhaps flowing in and energizing the Chakra. You can follow this procedure for each of the chakras changing the colours to those, which are appropriate for each different chakra, or if you feel that there is a particular chakra you wish to work on just hold your focus onto that specific one. Always ensure, once you are finished that your energies and consciousness is grounded by visualizing something like a tree root or taking your awareness to your feet and perhaps even wriggling them about. This ensures that you are back in the 'now' and that your focus is sufficient for you to continue with whatever you need to do next. This is especially important if you are intending to get into a car and drive or operate machinery. You could also work with a 'grounding' crystal such as Hematite or Snowflake Obsidian, which will help this process. Simply hold the crystal and visualize drawing the energy from the crystal up your arm, into your heart and see it circulating around the body, into the aura and down through the soles of your feet. This technique can be used at any time, not just after the Chakra balancing.

Crystals can work beautifully as tools to balance the chakras. Choosing 7 crystals - one for each major Chakra - is an excellent technique to provide for a general tune up during a healing session.

However, the combination chosen by the healer needs to be selected carefully. Many healers are guided by the traditional colours of the chakras and select crystals, which represent the appropriate colour of the Chakra such as:

| | | |
|---|---|---|
| Base - | Red Jasper - | Red |
| Sacral - | Carnelian - | Orange |
| Solar Plexus - | Golden Tigers Eye - | Yellow |
| Heart - | Aventurine/Rose Quartz - | Green/Pink |
| Throat - | Blue Lace Agate - | Light Blue |
| Brow - | Sodalite - | Indigo |
| Crown - | Amethyst/Clear Quartz - | Purple/Clear |

An alternative to the above is to consider using crystals, which are multi coloured such as Tourmaline for example which is bi or tri-coloured. Watermelon Tourmaline has a pink centre and a green outer ring. Would this colour combination work with the heart Chakra?

Diamonds, Clear Quartz, Apophylite etc hold the full spectrum of colour so may be good choices also.

Finally, another point of focus when selecting Chakra sets is to take into account the functions of the chakras and select a stone which you feel supports this role. Eg Rose Quartz is generally considered to promote unconditional love - does this make it a good choice for working with the heart centre?

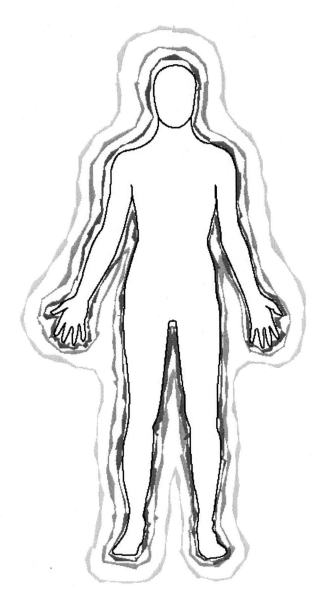

DIAGRAM 10 - Aura

# The Subtle Bodies / Aura

Contained within the aura or energy field around the body are the subtle bodies. Individual sections, which some clairvoyants perceive as different, coloured layers that correspond to each of the different chakras. This is a very simplistic way of viewing a complex manifestation, which is still open to conjecture between healers who have different perceptions of how the energy field is subject to change and what the responses are.

As a working model we can use the following as a simple guide:

THE ETHERIC BODY - this is the layer, which is most usually seen and is located very close to the physical body. Its corresponding Chakra is the BASE.

THE ASTRAL BODY - sometimes known as the EMOTIONAL BODY due to the fact that emotional upsets, shock, and resulting trauma can be held in this section of the energy field. Related Chakra is the SACRAL.

THE LOWER MENTAL BODY - linked into the SOLAR PLEXUS. This is the thinking or ego part of the body and is still very much a centre which the vast amount of humanity operate from (as opposed to the heart centre which is where we are now moving towards)
*These first three layers are connected to the personality within us. A lot of healers consider that it is within these three centres that many illnesses are based, as they are the most closely linked with our physical being.*

THE HIGHER MENTAL BODY - linked to the HEART Chakra and at this point we start to relate to others expressing love other than for the self for example. Some healers maintain that past life connections and trauma may be registered or held in this area.

THE INTUITIONAL BODY - connected to the THROAT Chakra. In this body we are thought to hold the template or blueprint of our consciousness. In other words, the perfect form that we aspire to.

THE SPIRITUAL BODY - linked to the BROW center and connecting us with higher spiritual awareness.

THE DIVINE BODY - linked to the CROWN Chakra and commonly accepted as connecting and allowing our divine consciousness to flow through us.

As healers, however, it is important to understand that the subtle bodies are one of the first places where disease and imbalances can be perceived and as these energy fields are extremely receptive to healing energy, it follows that we can help to prevent the manifestation of a physical illness or alleviate the presence of an illness by offering healing which can take the form of recharging, discharging, realigning, rebalancing or removal of energy blocks.

To connect with the energy bodies you can simply stand with a patient and run your hands through the auric field trying to detect changes in the density, temperature, texture etc. as you progress through each field. With practice you may be able to detect these imbalances etc. where the field has become damaged.

## Aura Brushing

It is possible to 'brush' the aura with crystals in order to cleanse and smooth the auric field. Simply get the patient to stand in a space where you can move around him or her. Then, with a crystal, starting at the crown, gently and slowly 'comb' the aura through by drawing the crystal down until you touch the ground.

As you pass through the aura you may encounter a slight 'stickiness' or feel that you wish to hold the crystal in a specific spot for a while. Just go with what feels right. When you reach the ground, let the crystal touch the ground and at that point visualize the negative energy being transmuted into the earth  a bit like putting manure on plants to make them grow! Then go back to the top of the crown and cover the front, back and sides. If the patient is lying on a couch, you can go over the front twice with the intent that one of the aura brushing processes is to cover the back or if you prefer you can crawl under the couch!

Many people respond to this treatment by saying that they are aware of a shimmer of energy or slight breeze. It is a good way of starting or finishing a treatment.

Although many diagrams illustrate the aura as a multi-layered egg, this is misleading, as it is perceived by many clairvoyants as energy fields which are multi-dimensional and which interpenetrate each other. These energy fields are constantly changing and shifting according to the outside influences such as those we encounter every day of our lives.

As healers we need to have a basic understanding or perception of the subtle bodies as many crystal healing techniques involve placing crystals within the auric field more so than on the physical body.

When working with crystals on the subtle bodies it is possible to link colour in addition to specific crystals so, for example, the etheric could be corresponded with red coloured crystals, the emotional body; yellow, mental body; orange, the astral body; pink, the causal body: light blue, the soul body; indigo and the spiritual body; purple, white or clear.

Alternatively, you may feel that you wish to simply place the crystals within the auric field wherever you intuit the imbalance to be or place the crystal on the relevant Chakra and visualise the energy flowing into the auric field via this point.

**Etheric Body** - No specified point of focus or placement point, as this body is completely interconnected with the physical.

**Emotional Body** - Stomach

**Lower Mental Body** - Left hemisphere of the brain. Place the stone or stones around the left side of the head. Check the correct position for each.

**Astral Body or Higher Mental Body** - Kidneys. Check to see if different stones are needed near each kidney or whether the same one is needed on both sides of the body. Tuck the appropriate stones under the back at about the level of elbow.

**Causal Body** - Medulla oblongata - at the back of the skull.

**Soul Body** - Pineal Gland. The easiest placement here is the centre of the forehead.

**Spiritual Body** - Pituitary Gland. Dowse for the best placement, which might be beside the head, level with the ears, behind the crown or at the forehead.

Another way of working with the subtle bodies is to balance simply the Physical, Mental, Emotional and Spiritual. In the classes that I have taught there is a very simple crystal layout or grid, which balances one or all of the bodies quite efficiently.

Ensure that the patient is lying down on the floor, couch or bed and is warm and comfortable.

Decide which body or combination of bodies you wish to align. Then, simply select the appropriate crystals to place in order to form the following symbols around the patient.

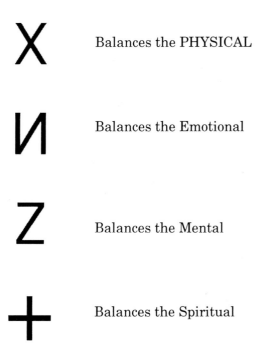

X        Balances the PHYSICAL

И        Balances the Emotional

Z        Balances the Mental

+        Balances the Spiritual

DIAGRAM 11

Starting with the Physical, simply place the crystals at the four end points and just trace the shape of the X across the body. If you wish to continue, overlay each symbol with the other until, if you decide to use all four symbols you will have 'drawn' a sort of sideways on Union Jack. As a healer it is

**69**

your responsibility to take care not only of your patient's energetic well being but also of your own. Many healers are extremely good at being able to give but find it difficult to receive. It is important to recognise that your increasing sensitivity will mean that you should receive regular healing sessions in order to keep you as pure a channel as possible.

These sessions can take the form of crystal healing but can also be any other therapy, which helps you to relax and release any negativity whether this is in the form of tiredness, stress, and fluctuating energy levels for example or in extreme cases psychic attack or negative influences.

It is preferable to receive these healing sessions from another therapist whom you know and are confident enough with to entrust your energy field.

In addition to this, if you can take the opportunity to talk over issues that crop up for you, this is an added bonus. From my own experience I have found that different perspectives other than my own can help to shed light on problems that I have encountered. Also talking over issues can help to release the emotions that sometimes crop up, helping us to see the problem and finally the solution more clearly but also more quickly.

If we take the view that a problem is really a lesson provided for our personal and spiritual growth, it follows that the faster we learn the lesson, the easier it becomes to leave it behind and move on.

As we grow spiritually, there is undoubtedly an increase in sensitivity. This can take any of the following forms (although this is by no means a definitive list!):

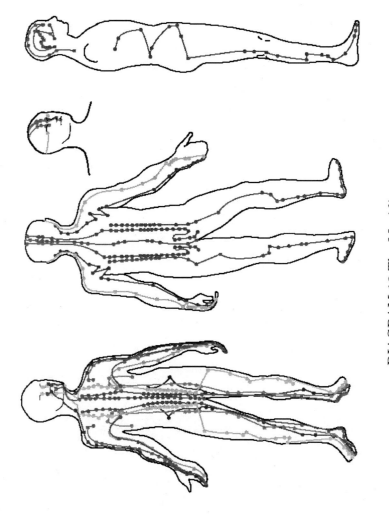

DIAGRAM 12 The Meridians

- Increased emotional responses
- Fluctuating energy levels
- Onset of allergic reactions such as diet, environment, noise
- Change in appetite and thirst
- Clearer awareness of reactions to atmospheres, places etc
- Change in sleep patterns
- Change in sexual energies
- Dislike of crowds, cities, pollution
- Vivid dreams
- Headaches or feeling of pressure around the head area
- Feeling disorientated, dizzy, slightly spaced out
- Difficulty in remembering things, muddled thought processes
- Increased awareness of the beauty of nature, music etc.
- Dawning realisation that some of the relationships or patterns in our lives we have maintained may be outdated and need to be changed or discontinued.

It is generally accepted that the group consciousness is beginning to shift and change. This will result in a greater amount of people finding that they are becoming aware of increased sensitivity, as well as psychic or spiritual awareness. As a healer, one of your functions is to learn to cope with this increase and teach your patients how to understand what is happening to them.

## Coping Mechanisms for Increased Sensitivity

1. *Keep a good balance in your life between work and play.*
You do not have to be a hermit wearing sackcloth and ashes to be a more effective healer. We are here to live our lives to the full and experience as much as possible. Try to ensure that you maintain a balance between your spiritual life and your ordinary life as well as keeping you grounded it also will

enable you to continue to identify with your patients more effectively if you maintain one foot in the real world. Ensure that you stay earthed and centred.

2. *Have a support system in place.*
By maintaining a network of colleagues who work in the healing field you can exchange ideas, perceptions, experiences and knowledge as well as receive support, advice and another perspective on the work that you are doing. It is extremely effective to be part of a group energy where you are not "in charge" but can be nurtured by the energy i.e. a regular meditation group for example. However, it is important to be selective and choose a group, which "feels" right.

3. *Be aware that your sensitivity will not be consistent. Avoid over stimulation.*
During times of spiritual growth we can feel less sensitive to the presence of guides and our intuitive abilities feel less strong. Recognise this as a growth pattern and have in place techniques such as dowsing, kinesiology etc., which help to underpin your healing so that you can maintain your confidence as a healer. Also recognise that during the more sensitive times you need to nurture yourself and try to avoid anything which might aggravate or stimulate the sensitivity.

Whenever we "open up" spiritually whether we are discussing spiritual matters, working as healers, meditating or simply reading a spiritual book our chakras open and quicken this can lead to a loss of energy - be aware of this and when necessary take measures to ensure that your energy does not dissipate.

Be careful who you discuss your work with your energy can be affected if you share it with others who are not in tune with you, be aware of the effects of reading newspapers or watching television when there are negative images and take steps to avoid them during sensitive times, avoid alcohol, drugs, chemically processed foods and materials, bright lights, noisy or smoky places etc. Nurture yourself.

4.*Become aware of the increased need for protection to your energy field.*
As your vibration raises people will become more aware of the energy, which you give off and will, at some level, be drawn to this. It is important to maintain your own space in order to ensure that you are not drained but also that your energy field is protected from negative influences.

Initially, all that may be required is that you strengthen your resilience by eating a healthy diet, getting sufficient rest and relaxation, avoiding stressful atmospheres, receiving healing on a regular basis, meditating, connecting with nature or simply having fun!

If you are not sufficiently protected you may find that you begin to feel depressed, de-motivated, lethargic, anxious, irritable, more aware of negative energy than positive energy. Some ways of counter-acting this are:

- Try wearing colours such as Orange which energizes, RoyalBlue which has a protective quality

- Work with symbols such as an equi-distant cross in a circle or visualise yourself in a protective egg or bubble you can combine colour into this visualisation to empower it even more

- Use crystals, which you have selected for their protective qualities (regularly cleansing and attuning them). Some traditional stones for protection are Golden Tigers Eye, Amethyst, Turquoise, and Lapis Lazuli but always use your own intuition.
- Work with particular essential oils, which have

again been selected for their protective qualities such as Rosemary, Patchouli etc.

- Try to ensure that wherever possible you place yourself in an uplifting environment. Watch a video which you know will make you laugh, listen to music that you find uplifting, make an effort to see friends who are good company.

- MOST IMPORTANT OF ALL, ASK YOUR GUIDES FOR MORE PROTECTION AND HELP.

IT IS IMPORTANT TO LOOK AT LOGICAL EXPLANATIONS FOR ANY SYMPTOMS WHICH OCCUR AND TO GET THEM CHECKED OUT BY A DOCTOR FIRST IF NECESSARY.

## What Are Meridians?

Over 5,000 years ago, the ancient Chinese discovered a subtle energy in the body that cant be seen, felt or found with the senses. They identified twelve acupuncture meridians, which are linked to a specific organ of the body, and it is along these meridians that an invisible nutritive energy, known to the Chinese as chi energy, travels through all living beings.

The energy enters the body through specific acupuncture points and flows to the organs, cells, and tissues, bringing a life-giving nourishment of a subtle energetic nature. The energy flow is not only found internally, but can be felt outside the external body and overtime, with practice and awareness they can be sensed with the hands, muscle testing techniques (kinesiology) or by dowsing.

Meridians are the pathways of the positive and negative energy power that flows through these 12 meridians, and they

Lung

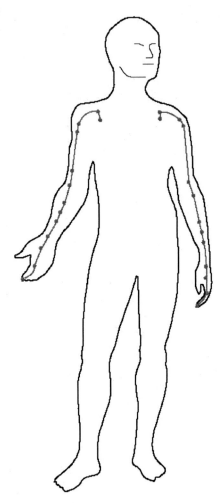

DIAGRAM 12a  Lung Meridian  directional flow starts from
the shoulder and ends at the thumb.  Positive emotions are
humility, tolerance and modesty. Negative emotions are
contempt and prejudice

Large Intestine

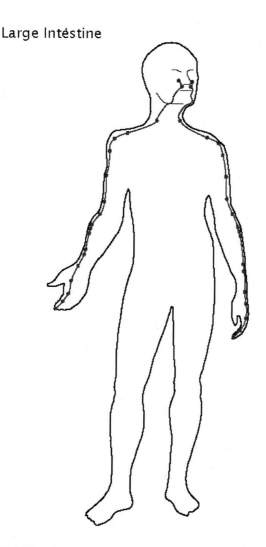

DIAGRAM 12b Large Intestine Meridian directional flow
starts at the face by the edge of the nostril and ends inside the
index finger. Positive emotions are self-worth and acceptance.
Negative state is guilt.

Spleen

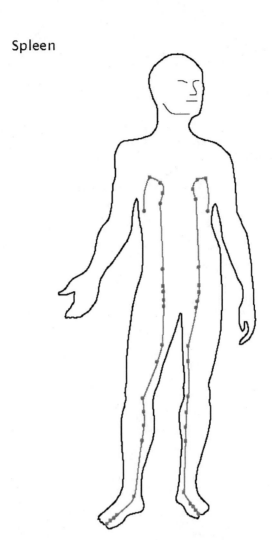

DIAGRAM 12c Spleen Meridian  directional flow starts at the
inside edge of the big toe and ends below the nipple by side of
chest.  Positive emotions are trust, confidence and security.
Negative emotions are fears about the future.

Stomach

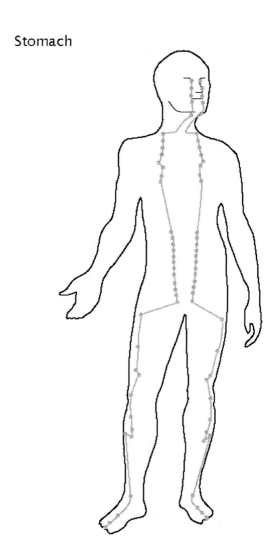

DIAGRAM 12d Stomach Meridian  directional flow starts at the inner edge of the eye orbit and ends at the outside of the second toe.  Positive emotions are contentment and tranquillity.  Negative emotions are greed, disgust, bitterness, nausea, hunger, desolation.

Heart

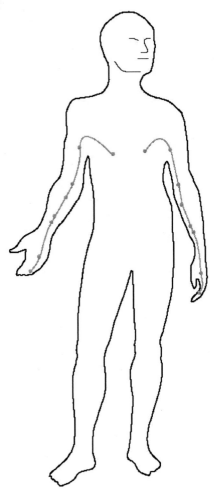

DIAGRAM 12e Heart Meridian  directional flow starts at the
front edge of the armpit and flows down to the inner side of
the little finger. Positive emotions are love and forgiveness.
Negative emotion is anger.

Small Intestine

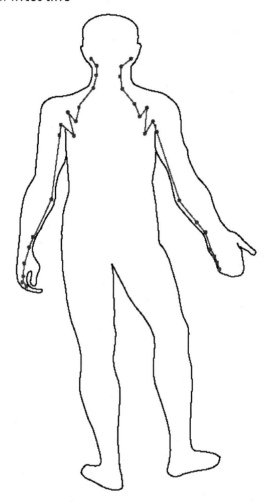

DIAGRAM 12f Small Intestine Meridian  directional flow at
the outside edge of the tip of the little finger and goes up to
the side of the ear by the cheek hollow.  Positive emotion is joy.
Negative emotion sorrow.

# Bladder

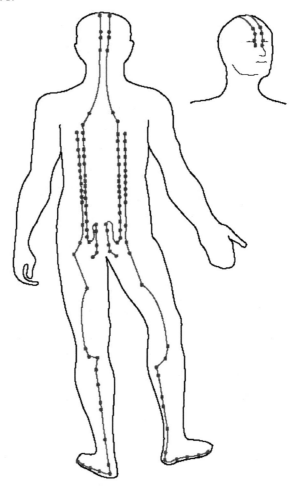

DIAGRAM 12g Bladder Meridian  directional flow at the
inner eye by the bridge of the nose and goes down to the
outside of the little toe.  Positive emotions peace and harmony.
Negative emotions are frustration and impatience.

Kidney

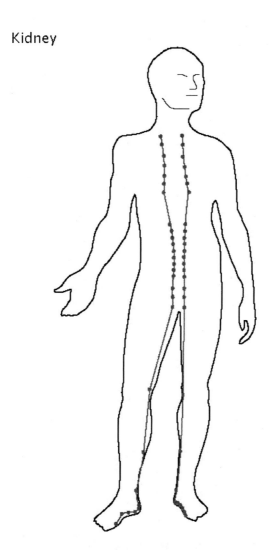

DIAGRAM 12h Kidney Meridian  directional flowat the ball of
the foot and goes up to where the collar and breast bone meet.
Positive emotions are sexual confidence.  Negative emotions
various sexual issues  lack of interest, lack of confidence in
sexual matters etc.

Liver

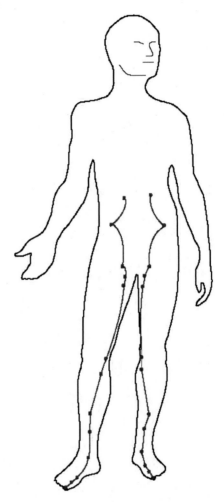

DIAGRAM 12i Liver Meridian  directional flow by the outside
of the big toe and rises to the bottom of the ribcage. Positive
emotions are positivity, cheerfulness.  Negative emotion is
unhappiness.

## Gall Bladder

DIAGRAM 12j Gall Bladder Meridian  directional flow from
the outer edge of the eye to the outer end of the fourth toe.
Positive emotions are love, forgiveness and adoration.
Negative emotions are fury and wrath.

# The Pericadium

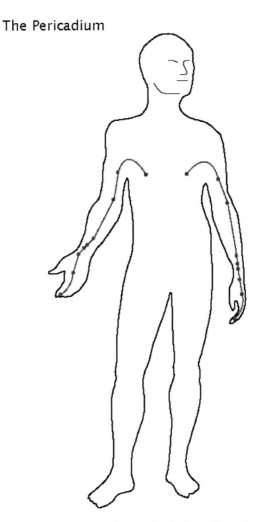

DIAGRAM 12k Pericardium Meridian  directional flow outer
edge of the nipple and goes down to the inside end of the
middle finger. Positive emotions are release, letting go of the
past, relationships etc., generosity.  Negative emotions are
jealousy, stubbornness, regret.

Triple Burner

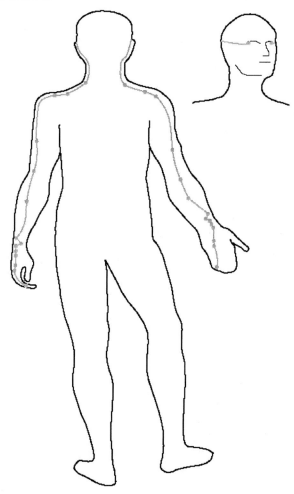

DIAGRAM 12l Triple Burner Meridian  directional flow starts at the ring finger on the outside edge and flows up to the outer edge of the eyebrow.  Positive emotions are elation and hope. Negative emotions are depression, sense of hopelessness, loneliness.

## Governing Vessel

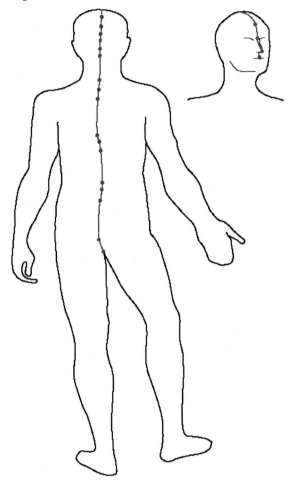

DIAGRAM 12m Governing Vessel Meridian  directional flow
starts at the tail bone and goes up the spine over the head to
the centre of the upper lip.  Specific emotional states are the
same as the Conception Vessel. This channel in conjunction
with the Conception Vessel below helps to maintain the flow of

Conception Vessel

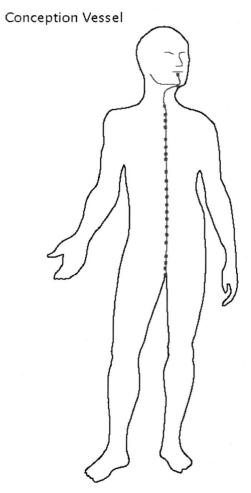

DIAGRAM 12n Conception Vessel directional flow starts at the perineum or base of the spine and goes up to the middle of the lower lip. Positive emotions are love, faith, courage. Negative emotions are fear, envy, hate. As with the Governing Vessel the Conception Vessel is considered to be the most important meridians as they maintain the flow of chI, prana or life-force energy through the whole of the body via the meridian system.

are all interlinked with each to make one continuous, unbroken flow, from one meridian to another in a specific order, with the energy flowing in one definite direction. Although, there is a continuous cycle, each meridian has its own characteristics and will perform specific functions for the organ that it is aligned too.

There are two major meridians known as the Conception Vessel and Governing Vessel, which supply the chi energy to the anterior and posterior mid line of the body.

Meridians are classified yin or yang on the basis of the direction in which they flow on the surface of the body.

## Yang
Yang energy flows from the sun, and yang meridians run from the fingers to the face or from the face to the feet. Yang represents: male, light, positive, external, hot, dry, active and strong and relates to the organs: stomach, small intestine, bladder, triple warmer, gall bladder, and large intestine.

## Yin
Yin energy, flows from the earth, and yin meridians flows from the feet to the torso, and from the torso along the inside (yin side) of the arms to the fingertips. Yin represents: female, dark, negative, internal, cold, wet, passive and gentle and relates to the organs: spleen, heart, kidney, circulation sex, liver, and lung,

## Energy Blockages

Energy blocks are created when the energy flow between all 12 meridians becomes interrupted and is not able to flow freely, resulting in an under energy in the remainder of the meridians.

DIAGRAM 13 Yin/Yang symbol

Imbalances in the meridians can be detected by using dowsing or manual muscle testing (kinesiology) which uses the bodys intelligence to non-invasively obtain information to establish where the blockage is and thus the over energy can be drawn out to re-establish a reconnection with the corresponding meridian and to ensure the bodys vitality remains in harmony.

## CoRRecting the EneRgy Blockage

To correct any blockage first identify where the blockage is occurring. You can dowse each meridian line either physically on the body or use the following diagrams

You can use the meridian chart to establish which meridian is blocked; you may establish there is more than one meridian blocked.

Once you have established which meridian you need to work on using a quartz point crystal you then move the flow of energy by tracing the meridian in the appropriate direction i.e. in the normal flow of the meridian. You may be aware of a slight stickiness or a feeling of resistance or you may simply feel that you wish to hold the crystal over a certain part of the meridian for a little longer. The crystal should be held about 10cms away from the body.

You should then go back and recheck the meridian flow to see if the blockage has cleared and then recheck other meridians to ensure that the flow is uniform and that the blockage has not just moved on. When using dowsing as a tool to diagnose it is important to remember that the result is dependant on you being neutral, you must not be tired, thirsty, or hungry it can affect the accuracy of your testing. It is also important that you practice dowsing, and to check each time that it is appropriate for you to dowse.

Finally, also be aware that a blockage in the meridian flow may be released by checking and rebalancing the chakras. Always check which procedure is more appropriate.

The meridian flow is activated 25 times each day and 25 times every night. Every two hours there is an energy surge into the appropriate organs as listed below:

| Meridian | Time |
|---|---|
| Gallbladder Meridian | 11pm – 1am |
| Liver Meridian | 1 am – 3 am |
| Lung Meridian | 3 am – 5 am |
| Colon Meridian | 5am – 7 am |
| Stomach Meridian | 7am – 9am |
| Spleen/Pancreas Meridian | 9am – 11 am |
| Heart Meridian | 11 am – 1 pm |
| Small Intestine Meridian | 1 pm – 3 pm |

| Bladder Meridian | 3 pm – 5 pm |
| Kidney Meridian | 5pm – 7 pm |
| Triple Heater Meridian | 7 pm – 9 pm |
| Endocrine Meridian | 9 pm – 11 pm |

## Barriers to Successful Healing

When working on others, it is possible to encounter barriers to healing which prevent you working as effectively as you feel you might. These barriers could be for a number of reasons such as the ones listed below and it is important for the therapist to be aware that these can sometimes crop up in order to try to break them down so that the healing can work to an optimum level.

Possible barriers, which a healer may encounter, could be:

Personality clash between the patient and healer
Lack of communication, patient and healer on the wrong wavelengths

Over identification between the patient and the healer - this can lead to a dependency upon the healer (or vice versa), which is inappropriate.

Differences in their belief structures whether it is professional, religious or personal beliefs.

Not wishing to be there (patient may have been "forced" to come to please a partner for example)

Lack of trust (either of the healer or the therapy)

Fear of criticism or judgment
Not being honest with the healer (patient may wish to impress the healer and give the answers that they think that

the healer wishes to hear rather than the truth)

Inability to communicate or connect with the healer e.g. personality clash, shyness on the part of the patient etc.

Fear of change - wishing to hold on to the illness/problem/ situation at some level and thereby reject the healing offered

Lack of respect for example patient may expect healer to be "special", however, if the healer falls short of this perception the patient may lose confidence in their ability. NB this is not a reason to encourage these perceptions in our patients!

Diversionary tactics - i.e. keeping a conversation going in order to "put off" the healing session.


## Conclusion

Now we seem to be at a point of change and transformation. Many channels and clairvoyants are aware of a change within the chakra systems of humanity. However, although many people are aware of these changes, we seem to be in a state of transition which makes it difficult for us to find common agreement on just how these changes will affect us as well as relatively basic information such as the colours and positions the chakras will ultimately evolve into.

I think that at the present time it is more important than ever to find our own truth and current level of awareness in order that we can continue with our personal and spiritual development on an individual basis. For a growing number of humanity it is no longer relevant to visualise opening and closing the chakras in the traditional ways. We need to recognise the transition stages that are occurring indicated by major life changes, developing psychic awareness, changes within personal belief systems, or simply a growing dissatisfaction with the way we live and perceive our lives and the lives of those around us.

Personal truth needs to be achieved, I believe, because currently humanity is shifting at a vast rate. Factors are increasingly being brought into play such as your spiritual path or life mission, implications of karma, willingness to move forward, as well as the influxes of energy, which have been pulsing the earth for some time and as a consequence have also affected the vibrationary rate of the planet and it's inhabitants. All these things will have a bearing as to development and growth of the new chakras. In time, I feel, that things will slow and a greater consensus of opinion will be available however, for now it is important for people to begin to learn to discern the stages that they are at as individuals and become more self empowered in order to move forward.

Crystal Therapy has a role to play in this. A skilled and intuitive therapist should be able to recognise transition stages, blocks to moving forward, etc. and provide the necessary, relevant treatment using Chakra sets, which may no longer relate to the traditional colour correspondence, for example to aid the process that their client is moving through.

# Chapter 5

# Meditations With Crystals

*One of the most effective ways to connect and begin to work with crystals is to meditate with them. This can be through visualization, following a set process or simply by just looking at the crystal for a period of time (this is sometimes known as scrying and is thought to enhance clairvoyant perceptions, it is probably one of the more widely known, stereotypical images that we in the west see relating to crystals, namely that of an exotically dressed clairvoyant sitting hunched, hands outstretched and gazing into a crystal ball in order to see the future!).*

## Earthing and Centreing

In order to work more effectively with crystals we need to ensure that we are thoroughly connected to the earth and centered.

Being earthed means that we have both feet on the ground and that we are alert and aware, that we are able to function effectively and interact with other people whether they are spiritually inclined or not as opposed to someone who is ungrounded, who is "spaced out", not able to maintain an interest or concentration on anything sufficiently.

Some people consider themselves to be spiritually superior if they are ungrounded and this is wrong. In order to be of "earthly use" we need to be able to communicate and function effectively with those people and situations we encounter. It is far more important that we learn to choose and control when it is appropriate to be a little ungrounded i.e. when we are meditating, healing etc and when it is not.

As well as being grounded we should be centered and by this we mean being able to connect with our personal sense of stillness, balance and strength, which is held within our being.

The following are some suggestions to help promote grounding and centering: -

a) Eating, drinking and (although not to be recommended) smoking, aid the grounding process. It is thought that particular foods such as meat, root vegetables etc. are more effective than other types of food.

b) Carrying out day-to-day tasks such as cleaning, ironing etc.

c) Gardening or simply getting in touch with nature.

d) Water - using it to drink, swim, shower, bathe or simply wash hands.

e) Physical exertion such as exercise which involves sweating, excreting help to release (bulimics who only vomit to release often have difficulty in earthing). Sporting activities help to anchor you into the body.

f) Therapies such as Reflexology, Massage and Shiatsu can help.

g) Visualisation techniques such as imagining you have magnets on your feet, seeing roots growing into the earth from your feet, visualising a column running through you linking you to heaven and earth etc.

h) Closing the chakras.

i) Using the breath to inhale earthing energy.

j)Using an earthing crystal maybe carnelian, snowflake obsidian,

k) Your partner - often you can see that there is one partner in a couple who has an earthing influence over the other.

l) Clapping hands, stamping feet, making sounds such as chanting.

m) Using appropriate essential oils. a) such as bergamot, frankincense, all citrus oils, peppermint, rosemary etc.


Experiment and find what works for you. Some of the above suggestions may have completely the opposite effect!

The following are some suggested meditations, which you could use in order to help you to connect more deeply with crystals. I would suggest that you find the ones that you like and record it or memorize it in order that you can relax more fully.

Should you choose to read a meditation to a group, I would suggest that you work with the meditations with which you feel comfortable reading as if you work with words, which you find difficult to say, or visualizations, which are not your style, your discomfort will be apparent to those listening.

# IMPORTANT NOTES:

1. Before commencing any work with crystals always ensure that they have been cleansed and dedicated to the highest and purest good.

2. You may wish to light candles to signify working with light as well as burning incense or essential oils. You may also wish to play some gently relaxing music in the background.

3. You may wish to have a pen and paper to make notes of any responses, which come up. It is helpful sometimes to keep a record of responses to meditations and to track how they change from time to time according to what is happening to you.

4. It is a good idea to try to unravel the symbolism of your responses to some of the meditations. There are many books on dreams, which can help to provide clues to the symbolic relevance to visions, which your subconscious may project during meditations.

5. Try to ensure that callers, telephones, family etc will not interrupt you.

6. You may wish to have a grounding crystal to hand for use at the end of the meditation.

7. At the end of the meditation, once you have finished, always cleanse the crystal again.

## Meditation 1   Connecting With the Energy of the Crystal

Hold your crystal in your hand. Sit or lie in the most comfortable position for you.

Sit or lie comfortably holding the cleansed crystal in your hand. Take in 3 deep breaths, sighing out loudly to release tension and ground your energy. Release any points of tension, cough or clear your throat and shift your body in order to be as comfortable and relaxed as you possibly can.

With your eyes closed, start to move the crystal around your hand with your fingers. Feel the shape and texture of the crystal. Does it have any chips or holes? Is it smooth or rough? What temperature is the crystal is it warmer or cooler than you would expect it to be?  Is it lighter or heavier than you expected?

In your minds eye or brow Chakra, try to visualize the colour of the crystal. What do you feel the colour of the crystal represents?

Then take your awareness back to the crystal in your hand and begin to visualize the crystalline energy begin to activate and send this energy up your arm, into your shoulder and down into the heart Chakra.

You may be aware of the energy 'buzzing' or tingling as it begins to flow up, a heightened emotional state, the temperature of the crystal being cooler or hotter than you would expect or simply a strong colour in the 3rd eye or brow center. Just allow this process to continue.

When you feel that the crystal energy has reached the heart Chakra begin to visualize the energy being beamed from the heart center out into your auric field. Surrounding and

**100**

encompassing you with the energetic vibrations of this particular crystal.

Sit for as long as you wish, allowing any perceptions whether they are physical, mental, emotional or even spiritual responses to occur.

When you are ready, honour and acknowledge your experiences with the crystal, you may wish to thank the crystal for what you have perceived. Then slowly reverse the process, allowing the energy to filter back into your heart center retaining any that you may require for personal healing etc.). Then allowing the flow to continue back into the shoulder, down the arm and back into the crystal.

Slowly bring your focus back into the room, become aware of your breathing and begin to breathe more deeply. Feel your feet on the floor and when you are ready, open your eyes.

Make notes if you wish and then cleanse the crystal again.

## Meðitation 2. Connecting With The Crystal Keeper Or Deva

Sit or lie comfortably and focus on your breathing. Holding the crystal that you wish to work with. Taking your focus to the 3rd eye or brow center become aware of a garden or a warm meadow on a summers day. Start to walk, noticing all the colours of the wild flowers, which greet you as you pass by. Ahead, in the distance, there is a wall, which has a wooden door. You walk towards the wooden door and gently it opens as if to beckon you inside.

Carefully you walk through the door, inside there is another garden but this time it is secluded and quieter. The flowers in the garden are all the same colour, the colour of the crystal that you have in your hand. Suddenly you become aware of a cave, you walk to the cave, go inside and once inside you see the walls are made of your crystal. There is a comfortable seat in the center of the cave that you go to and sit upon. Sit for a moment feeling the energy of the crystal, surrounding and encompassing you until you become aware of a powerful yet gentle presence. It is the deva or keeper of the crystal that you hold. Stay for a moment or as long as you wish in the company of this being. Allow the deva to communicate in whatever way is most appropriate to you the quality or gift that this crystal holds for you.

Eventually, it is time to leave. Honour and acknowledge the connection you have made and slowly rise from the seat in the cave and make your way out into the secluded garden, through the wooden door and back into the meadow or garden.

Gently start to bring your focus back into the room where you are and become aware of your feet on the ground, seeing roots growing out of the soles of you feet and anchoring you to the ground. When you are ready open your eyes and if you wish make notes of your experiences.

## Meditation 3. Self Healing With Crystal Terminations or Points

*This is a very simple meditation/visualization for which you need 2 Quartz points or terminations.*

Hold the crystals, one in each hand. In one hand, hold the termination so that the point is facing up towards the arm, in the other have the point facing out, away from the arm.

Then closing your eyes and ensuring that you are comfortable, visualize drawing energy into the crystal which points

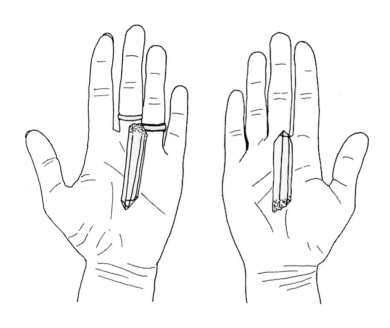

DIAGRAM 14 - hands with crystal points

towards the body. You may wish to see this as light or a colour or simply an energy. Go with whatever feels right for you. Be aware of the energy flowing up your arm, along the shoulder and down into the heart. Allow it then to flow throughout the body, see it flushing any blockages of energy and allow them to flow through and out of the body. This process is helped by the crystal that you are holding in the other hand, which is pointing away from the body. As the energy starts to reach this crystal it becomes activated and starts to help to draw the old energy from the body as the other crystal allows new energy to flow into the body.

Just keep this process going until you feel that you are ready to stop. At this point, put the inward flowing crystal down but allow the outward flowing crystal to continue to release the old negative energy.

See or ask that this old, negative energy be transmuted and cleansed within the earth and start to bring your focus back into the room. Ensure that both crystals are thoroughly cleansed before putting them away.

## Meδítatíon 4.   Chakra Balancíng Vísulísatíons

As we discussed in the previous chapter, the health of an area of the physical body and the condition of its associated Chakra are considered interdependent eg: when a Chakra is clear and vital, the associated portions of the body should also be in an optimum state. As chakras are cleared, vitalized and expanded in clarity and development, one may experience the actualization of qualities, which have not been manifest. These meditations will be complimented by the additional use of holding a clear quartz crystal during the meditation.

# Meditation:

Take your awareness to the *Base Chakra* that is located in the area of the base of the spine in the area of the lumber. It is the center of vitality, physical energy and self-preservation. It activates and strengthens the will to live, to survive, to manifest etc., assisting one to live on the spiritual plane and stimulates life-sustaining energies. It is the center that vitalizes the kidneys, the supernal glands and the spinal column in the physical body. The colours associated with the base Chakra are red. *Imagine the colour red pouring into the base Chakra, be aware of the center opening to receive more of this vibrant colour and see or feel the Chakra starting to expand and grow, allowing a greater flow of energy than before.*

The *Sacral Chakra* is next and is located in the area 1 or 2 inches below the navel, it is the center of desire, emotion, creativity and sexuality. It stimulates the creative life force, which is required for existence on the physical plane. This center vitalizes the digestive system, reproductive organs, sexual activity and the areas where hormones are produced. The colour associated with this Chakra is orange. *Imagine the vibrant colour of orange and send this colour to the Sacral Chakra. Visualize the colour opening this center and realigning and balancing the center. Allow the sacral Chakra to expand and the energy flow to increase.*

The *Solar Plexus Chakra* is located at the solar plexus area, below the breastbone and behind the stomach. It is sometimes considered to be located at the navel. This center is linked to personal power (ego), ambition, intellect, desire and emotions based on intellect. Physically, it is linked to the well being of the stomach, gall bladder, sympathetic nervous system (activating involuntary muscles which enhance the mobilization of the physical body), pancreas, and adrenal glands. The associated colour is yellow. *Moving up to the Solar*

*Plexus Chakra, see the clear, bright colour yellow flowing into this Chakra. Allowing the Chakra to expand to an even greater degree, see this Chakra as the energetic mouth of the body, which takes in prana, chi or life force energy and passes it throughout the body via the meridian system. Take a moment to allow this increase of energy to permeate the body.*

The next Chakra is the *Heart Chakra*; its location is in the center of the chest at the level of the heart. It is the center of compassion, love and group consciousness. Its the center, which energises the heart, thymus, circulatory system, blood and cellular structure. The colours of the heart center are pale green or sometimes pink. *Allow the flow to continue up into the heart center. See the colours of pink, green or a merging of both colours start to flow into this center. Try to feel the physical expansion of this center as it takes in more energy and increases its power.*

Move now up to the *Throat Chakra* that is located at the neck, the center being recognized as the area of the throat, located above the collarbone. It is the center of communication, sound and expression of creativity via thought, speech and writing. It acts to provide for the understanding of both verbal and mental communications. It physically is the center, which vitalizes the thyroid gland, throat and jaw areas, alimentary canal, lungs, vocal cords and the breath. The colour associated with this center is light blue. *See the Throat Chakra responding as you direct the clear light blue to it. Drawing upon the blue to increase the size of this Chakra and allow for a greater flow of energy.*

The next Chakra is known as the *Brow or Third Eye Chakra.* It is located in between and just above the eyebrows. It is the center of psychic power and higher intuition. It is the center that physically addresses the cerebellum, nose, central nervous system, the pituitary gland and the left eye. It is believed that the combined interaction of the pineal and pituitary glands activates this center. The associated colour is Indigo. *Visualise a deep powerful blue indigo lighting up this center, flowing and expanding it to allow a greater amount of energy to pass through thereby ensuring an empowered Brow Centre.*

The final Chakra is the *Crown.* It is located at the crown of the head and is known as the center relating to spirituality, enlightenment and dynamic thought. Physically, this center energises the cerebrum, the right eye and the pineal gland. Its colour associations are purple, white or white gold. *Finally, take your awareness to the Crown Centre. From a space high above draw down the colours you feel most appropriate, white, purple or white gold. You may wish to mix the colours go with whatever you feel you wish to do. As this center expands take a moment to sit in perfect balance with each center drawing on its appropriate colour, creating an individual rainbow of colours within you.*

## Meditation 4  Individual Colour Meditations

Again, the meditation experience will be enhanced if you hold a specific crystal that is the same colour as the colour worked with in the meditation.

## Red Meditation

Relax and close your eyes.

Take in 3 deep breaths, sighing out to release any tension and aid the grounding process.

In your mind's eye see yourself walking down a country path that leads you to a field of red poppies swaying in the summer breeze.

You find a clearing amongst the poppies where there lays a red blanket, gently lie down on the blanket.

Take your focus to the sun, which has begun to set.

As it starts to sink below the horizon, the sky becomes ablaze with colour. It is filled with all the hues and shades of the colour red.

The colours are alive and dancing, let them gently caress and surround your physical body.

Sense how this colour affects you mentally, physically and spiritually.

Relax in this space for a while until the sound of my voice brings you back.

Now gently let the energy begin to recede as the scene slowly fades and your attention brings you back into the room.

Feel the weight of your body in the chair and become aware of your breathing. When you are ready, open your eyes.

## Orange Meditation

Relax and close your eyes.

Take in 3 deep breaths, sighing out and releasing any tension. Feel the breaths aiding the grounding process.

In your mind's eye, see yourself standing before an orange curtain, pull the curtain aside and find yourself entering a room that is glowing from the flames of a flickering burning log fire.

In front of the fire is an orange rug, go forwards and take your place on the rug.

Watch the flames dancing together creating the full orange spectrum of colours.

Feel the energy of the colours radiating from the fire, swirling and filling your aura. Let yourself go as the energies merge and you begin to sense the qualities and properties of orange and the colour connects with you.

Sit in this energy and maintain the connection until the sound of my voice brings you back.

Now gently, let the energy begin to recede as the scene slowly fades and your attention brings you back into the room.

Feel the weight of your body in the chair and become aware of your breathing. When you are ready, open your eyes.

## Yellow Meditation

Relax, close your eyes.

Take in 3 deep breaths sighing out to release any tension and to aid the grounding process.

See yourself standing in a white corridor leading to a YELLOW door.

Walk towards the door, open it and enter.

You walk into room bathed in yellow sunlight. Over by the window there is a softly padded yellow seat. You walk to the seat and sit down. Become aware of the soft cushions gently merging with your physical form, melting into one and encompassing you within and energetic embrace of yellow.

Turn your face towards the window and feel the vibrant morning sunlight warm your face as it beams into the room. Outside the window what do you see? Fields of golden corn, smiling sunflowers returning your stare or maybe groups of spring-like daffodils? Take a moment to visualise your symbolic representation of yellow. As you view this picture, your senses continue to expand, opening your awareness up to so much more.

Become aware of the energy starting to radiate around you as it brings forward the qualities and properties of yellow and allow your intuition to connect with the force of this colour until you start to gain an understanding of the qualities that yellow brings forward. These qualities may be positive, negative or both. Simply accept what you are given.

PAUSE

Know that your time in this magical room is limited and that you must now return back. Allow the scene to fade along with the yellow vibration that you have attuned to and begin to bring yourself back into this room. Feeling the weight of your body on the chair and sensing the rise and fall of your chest as you become aware of your breathing. When you are ready open your eyes and write down what you were given for yellow.

## Pink Meditation

Relax and close your eyes.

Take in 3 deep breaths, sighing out to release any tension and to aid the grounding process.

You are in a garden as the sun begins to set. You become aware of the vibrant pinks illuminated in the sky which cast a glow around the garden that you are in. The air is warm and fragrant, smelling of the soft pink roses, which surround you. Sit for a moment basking in the pink glow that surrounds and encompasses you. Experience the peace of this moment.

Then, as quickly as this moment was created it begins to fade as the golden sun starts to set and the intense pink starts to recede into the night.

It is time to return. Become aware again of your breathing and your body in its physical form. When you are ready bring your focus back into the room and open your eyes, ensuring that you are fully grounded and centred.

## Green Meditation

Relax and close your eyes.

Take in 3 deep breaths, sighing out to release any tension and to aid the grounding process.

Imagine yourself walking through a meadow carpeted with fresh green grass.

As you walk you come to a cluster of trees, you lie beneath one of the trees gently nestling your body on a bed of soft green ferns.

You look up and see the varying colours of the green leaves dappled by the watery rays of the sun.

As you lie here become aware of the green energy gently pulsating around you and flowing into your auric field.

Feel yourself become at one with the energy as it connects with you and brings forward the qualities that the colour green holds for you.

Relax in the place until the sound of my voice brings you back.

Now gently let the energy begin to recede as the scene slowly fades and your attention brings you back into the room.

Feel the weight of your body in the chair and become aware of your breathing. When you are ready open your eyes.

## Blue Meditation

Relax and close your eyes.

Take in 3 deep breaths, sighing out to release any tension and to aid the grounding process.

See your self on a clear, warm spring afternoon, walking through a wood carpeted with bluebells.

See the clear blue sky suspended above you.

As you walk you see a clearing, in the clearing is a blue cushion. Take yourself to it and gently sit down, become relaxed as the colours begin to surround and merge with your body.

Be aware of the bluebells surrounding you, feel the softness of the petals encompassing you, sense blue rays radiating from the petals and merging with your aura.

Feel the energy flowing as the colour connects and bonds with you.

Stay and relax in this place as you gain an understanding of what the colour blue brings for you at this moment.

Now, gently let the image begin to fade and feel your awareness returning as you become connected and grounded with the earth and your attention returns to the room.

Feel the weight of your body in the chair and become aware of your breathing. When you are ready, open your eyes.

## Indigo Meditation

Relax and close your eyes.

Take in 3 deep breaths, sighing out to release any tension and to aid the grounding process.

See yourself walking along a moonlit path under the indigo night sky.

As you walk, you discover a lake only the reflection of the moon illuminates the dark stillness of the water.

You become aware of an indigo cloak that has been placed around your shoulders and as you feel the cool night breeze you draw it closer to your body.

Stand for a while and gaze into the water and feel the cloaks energy radiating around you.

Become aware of the energetic presence of the colour indigo connecting with you.

Allow yourself to connect with the force of this colour as you gain an understanding of the energy it brings.

Stay in this magical space until the sound of my voice brings you back.

Now gently let the energy begin to recede as the scene slowly fades and your attention brings you back into the room.

Feel the weight of your body in the chair and become aware of your breathing. When you are ready open your eyes.

## Puaple Meδítatíon

Relax and close your eyes.

Take in 3 deep breaths, sighing out to release any tension and to aid the grounding process.

Imagine that you are walking along a garden path just as the sun starts to go down. The garden is ablaze with purple coloured flowers, deeply perfumed with a scent not unlike that of Frankincense. You become aware of a slight chill and ahead, lying on a seat is a cloak of the deepest, richest purple. You walk towards it and place the cloak around you. It has a hood, which you pull up over your head.

The robe is warm and welcoming and as you draw it more closely around you are aware that the colour is blending into your energy field. The perfume of the flowers become more intense as you connect deeply to the colour purple, feeling a sense of power and dignity which connects to this spiritual and powerful colour.

Sit for a moment, experiencing the connection to your own personal power and spirit.

When you are ready, take off the robe and leave it upon the seat.

Become aware of the weight of your body on the chair and in your own time start to bring your focus back into the room, ensuring that you are centred and grounded.

# Chapter 6

# How To Start Working With Crystals

When you start to work on others with crystals it is important that you ensure that you are in an appropriate mood and that you are grounded and centred. As the healer, it is important to acknowledge that the roles that you play in the healing session is going to be adversely affected if you are stressed, angry or uptight. Try to be aware of the needs of the patient it may be worth asking yourself the following questions during the session:

Have I prepared both the room and myself energetically for this session? In other words, am I grounded, centered and relaxed? Are my crystals cleansed and ready to work? Is the room warm and comfortably lit and the energy of the room cleansed and prepared for healing? Perhaps by lighting a candle to signify working with light energy and an incense stick or appropriate essential oil (such as lavender, frankincense or rose) burning to maintain a cleansing within the room as you work.

Have I put my patient at ease?

Have I gained a good idea of what the patient wants to achieve from this session? (Ask open ended questions these begin with What, Why, Where, Which, When and How. It is virtually impossible for your patient to answer any question with a one word answer when you begin a sentence with any of these words)

Am I allowing myself time to earth and then connect with guides, crystal energy etc.?

Am I paying sufficient attention to the responses of my patient during the session always be aware of the needs of your patient and stop the treatment if they appear to be distressed or uncomfortable.

Have I agreed in advance to give a sufficiently clear indication that the session has been completed so that the patient is able to relax completely into the session? Usually a light pressure on the shoulders or stroking the feet can do this these techniques have the additional benefits of helping to ground the patient.

Have I ensured that the patient is sufficiently grounded before allowing them to stand up? Perhaps by offering them a drink of water.

Have I set aside enough time to discuss and record feedback if necessary?

Always ensure that you have a ready supply of water, glasses, tissues, mints or cough sweets pen and paper and of course your diary to arrange another appointment if necessary, to hand.

There are many ways that crystals can be used. They encourage everyone to be creative and even now I am constantly surprised at the different and innovative ideas that inspire people to incorporate crystals into their lives.

# Self-healing Techniques With Crystals

1. Place a crystal on a specific Chakra and simply breathe in the energy.

2. Chant or simply breathe into a crystal and allow the vibrating out breath returning from the crystal to bathe you with its energy.

3. Wear a crystal to protect and energise the aura.

4. Sleep with crystal in order to enhance dreams but can also provide deep healing during sleep and perhaps another perspective to problems. Keep a notepad and pen by the side of the bed so that you can record details of the dreams whilst they are still fresh in your mind.

5. Energise water with crystals to create a gem elixir - see below.

6. Self-healing by self knowledge. Notice which crystals you are drawn to and look at the qualities that they hold within them. These qualities may provide a mirror for youself.

7. Place a crystal in bath water (ensure that it will not be adversely affected by the water first!) and bathe in the energized water.

8. Place a piece of Rose Quartz by microwaves, computers, TVs etc in order to reduce or clear the electromagnetic fields that are given out.

9. Place a small tumblestone in your mobile phone to counteract the microwaves when using it.

10. Keep a specific crystal for meditation or to bring you to a point of focus. Perhaps create an altar on which you can place

photographs of loved ones etc.

11. Animals respond well to crystals. Give them energized water (with the crystal removed!) or treat them with gem essences.

12. Place a crystal in the room to enhance the qualities that you wish to bring into the room. For example use a stone, which is good for concentration such as pyrite, in the study or by the computer, and place a stone such as Rose Quartz, which harmonizes and radiates unconditional love in the living room.

13. Crystals can be used as energisers to enhance vitamins, medicines, food, water, even face creams etc.

14. To help channel creativity dedicate a crystal to helping with creative thoughts and abilities whether it is writing a book, painting a picture or simply writing a letter etc.

15. Allow children to play with crystals. They are usually very intuitive in selecting the crystal, which is right for them and can be useful in helping them go to bed for instance but they can also be used creatively by allowing the child to make patterns with the crystals that can form a Mandala. (Mandala is a Sanskrit word meaning circle and is a symbolic diagram which is said to represent humanities connection with the Cosmos)

16. It may be possible to boost batteries for torches etc by placing the crystal overnight near to or touching the battery.

17. At work, crystals on the desk can double as a paperweight but be used as points of focus, protection, energisers etc.

18. As gifts. It is thought that the most important crystals are received as gifts from others.

DIAGRAM 15 - mandala

19. As a source of comfort crystals can offer love and companionship on a different level

20. They can be used as a focus point during tiresome jobs such as ironing etc. Carry crystals and place it at eye level. Use to draw energy and power to continue with the work in hand

21. Spiritual development. Using crystals in meditation can carry you into a deeper state and can help to develop the third eye.

22. Healing. Keep some tumble stones and select one daily, which you can carry around with you.

23. Can help to form a telepathic link with a loved one from whom you are separated.

24. Crystals can help you discord or disconnect from someone i.e. to finish a relationship amicably, perhaps by giving the crystal as a final offering.

25. Creating a mandala in the garden that could perhaps be dedicated to healing the earth by connecting with lunar and solar energies and drawing them into the earth.

26. When doing any form of healing which is to be directed at the physical body find an anatomical picture of the healthy body part you are sending the healing to and use this to enhance your visualisation.

## Absent Healing

It is possible and also highly effective to send healing to a person when they are not present in the room with you. This is known as absent healing.

It is important NOT to send healing without the prior agreement of the person to who it is being sent. In exceptional circumstances such as when a patient is unconscious, I ask that the healing be sent to the Higher Self of the patient and to be taken if appropriate otherwise I ask that the Higher Self sends on the healing to a person, place or situation more appropriate to receive it or to simply transmute the healing into the earth.

The other point to remember before starting to send healing absently is that the energetic connection between patient and healer is very strong but that there is no verbal or body language to alert us to what is actually going on. Therefore it is vital that when working in this way we pay the utmost attention to personal protection and also emphasise that the healing be carried for the highest good of all and the harm of none.

When working on a patient absently, we need to ensure that we have their permission to carry this out and that they wish us to send healing to them. It is also more effective to have what is known as a 'witness' to work with. This is something connected to the patient which carries the energy signature of the person you are sending the healing to. It may be as simple as a piece of paper with their written signature, something which belongs to them such as a watch or item of jewellery, a nail clipping or piece of their hair. Generally, I use the following outline and ask patients to sign inside the outline. This means that I can also write what crystals I have used and how I felt the session progressed and this can be shown, given or discussed with the patient at an appropriate time following the session.

*If you are working with energetic signatures such as hair, jewellery etc. you can place them in the center of the diagram when working.*

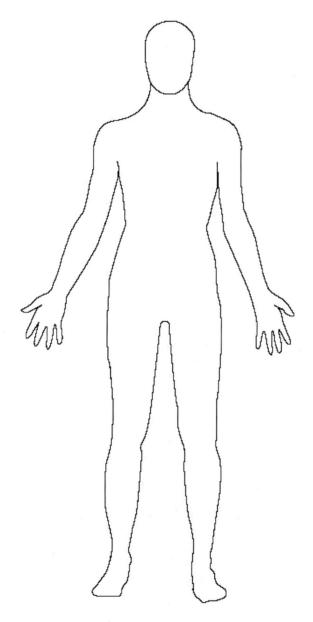

DIAGRAM 16 Blank body outline for absent healing

# Using Clear Quartz Points

*Clear quartz points have a directional flow to the point, that end being the focus of direct energy flow and the other end of the crystal having a 'drawing away' effect.*

When using points they can be used as follows:

TERMINATIONS POINTING UPWARDS:- Place crystals in opposite directions – this splits the directional flow of the energy in half.

UNGROUNDING: - Raises consciousness, strengthening male energy line, cleansing and straightening

TERMINATIONS POINTING DOWNWARDS GROUNDING: - Cleansing and straightening. Crystal points placed in a downward direction towards earth  brings a quality to the energy flow which is  then continue with cleansing and straightening.

GEM ESSENCES
Gem essences are energized water, which carry the energy signature of a crystal.

Water in itself is a truly amazing medium to work with. Experiments carried out are beginning to show that water has an ability to hold information. For example, a single snowflake consists of  billions upon billions of water molecules, which are arranged in a specific way, each snowflake is individual and does not match any other. When a snowflake has been allowed to melt and refreeze under the same conditions, it will reform in exactly the same pattern as it held previously.

Even more interesting were experiments carried out by a French biochemist called Jacques Benveniste. As recently as the 1990s, he was asked to run a series of trials that originally were requested in order to disprove homeopathy. During these tests he experimented with water in a glass, underneath which and outside of, an aspirin was placed. Using a copper coil as a conductor, he discovered, much to his surprise, that the water carried a recordable energetic signature of the aspirin within itself. He has subsequently devoted a great deal of his time to proving the theory that water has an ability to hold memory much to the disgust of more conventional scientists.

Using water, crystal or gem essences can be made in various ways but they are usually simply made by placing a crystal in water and allowing the water to draw upon and retain the crystals energetic imprint.

This work has been further developed by Dr Masaru Emoto who has found that polluted or treated water or water exposed to negative emotions such as anger, fear etc forms distorted random crystalline structures when frozen. On the other hand, water which is pure and has been exposed to positive emotions when frozen, forms beautifully ordered geometric designs.

When we consider that the brain is 85% water and this water is able to hold energetic memories, it places a different perspective on what skills are at the disposal of a healer. Perhaps, one of the healer's skills should be the ability to re-programme the memory locked with the water contained in the human body.

Pure spring water is preferable and clear glass bowls should be used, it is important that there is no written or imprinted letters, numbers or symbols within the glass utensils that you use as this can affect the purity of the energy which you are seeking to contain within the essence.

Ideally, the gemstone should be placed in direct sunlight as this process in conjunction with the innate ability of water to retain the energy signature combines to create a powerful energetic imprint, which can be used in many ways. Brandy (or other forms of alcohol) can be used in order to preserve the contents of the bottle over a long term basis.

Although the majority of crystals can be safely used to energise water it is important to note that there are varieties of crystals, which are toxic or soluble in water and so great, care should be taken when choosing crystals to prepare gem essences. A general rule of thumb is that the quartz family is safe but softer crystals such as calcite and Selenite are water soluble and should not be placed in water.

Most people assume that flower and gem essences should be taken orally but they can be used in a variety of ways:

In the bath.
Sprayed into the aura this is considered the most beneficial and powerful way of taking them.
Rubbed on pulse or acupuncture points.
Sprayed into the room.
Placed upon the crown or other Chakra points.
Drunk in water.
Used absently.

The energized water can also be used to water plants and for pets to drink.

As with crystals they are a very creative medium, which can greatly enhance the healing process. They can be deceptively powerful and as with most vibrational remedies need to be used with respect and honour.

# Pyramid Exercise

Using crystals to create a safe space is an ideal way to accentuate the healing process or simply to provide a refuge where the energy can be attuned to the patients' individual requirements. It is a relatively simple procedure that is extremely flexible and can be used in a variety of situations.

The geometrical shape of the pyramid has been prized in the past by many ancient civilizations but even today, mathematicians and scientists as well as those of a more esoteric nature are convinced that there is great significance held within the shape.

Edgar Cayce, who imparted information through deep trance, claimed that the Great Pyramid had been built with the assistance of the Atlanteans. They were thought to have used their highly developed mental powers to place the stones, by levitation, in specific positions. It has been claimed the measurements of the pyramid gave and continue to give, information concerning the future of mankind by foretelling events to come. This, of course, ties in with the information that scientists and mathematicians are now decoding.

For this exercise all that is needed are 2 crystals of identical type and a seat for your patient.

Cleanse the crystals and when the patient is seated comfortably on the chair, place the crystals one at the front and one at the back of the seat. Try to estimate the size of the pyramid and height - be guided by the height of the patient.

Stand facing the side of the patient and place the palms of the hands over or at an angle to the crystals. Attune to the light and ask that the patient receive that which is appropriate at this moment in time.

Maintaining your link, wait until you receive some form of communication from the crystal - this could be heat, cold, vibration etc. - then ask for an ETHERIC crystal to appear. This should come out of the air, above the head of the patient.

When you are ready, "draw" the energy from the crystals you have placed on the floor up to the etheric crystal visualising them joining. Do this 3 times and then step back.
Allow the energy to build and then start to check that the shape is uniform and that the energy is equal. If it is not, channel some universal energy from your hands to help the process along.

At this point, the patient can be left in the sacred space to meditate or can be given healing. You may well find that any healing given is more powerful than without the pyramid.

It is important tot note that although the healer can move in and out of the pyramid space, no other person should "invade" the space. The space needs to be dismantled before the patient is allowed to move out of it.

To remove the pyramid, offer the etheric crystal back to the Universe, visualising the process, acknowledge and give thanks.

Check for any residual energy and gently return the energy back to the crystals placed on the floor.

Finally, cleanse the crystals that you have used and ground the patient.

# Chapter 7

# Advanced Techniques

Working with crystals on a deeper, more profound level often brings up or highlights issues that need to be addressed. This can be in the form of a growing need to move on from outmoded thought patterns, relationships or simply to accept a general change in the way that we perceive the world.

Phyllis Krystal is a trained psychotherapist who in her book entitled *"Cutting The Ties That Bind"* develops the idea that we can and should liberate ourselves from outmoded relationships, thought forms, places, situations in order to progress on both spiritual but also personal levels.

In the book she details various methods of disconnecting from these ties which can encompass working with complex relationships between parent and child, partners, friends etc. in addition to the relationship that we have with ourselves.

Some clairvoyants describe these ties as actual bonds between those involved which can constantly affect the energy (both positively and negatively) of those linked.

It follows therefore that any outmoded, negative attachments, which stifle and sap the energy of a person should be disconnected. Some consider an exception to this is the link between parent and child that should be maintained until around the age of 18 for the sake of the child.

It is recommended that you read Phyllis Krystal's book but as healer's we can see that it is sometimes necessary to support our clients through the process of tie cutting.

This can be done with visualisation and with the addition of crystals forming a complementary grid.

Working with symbols can enhance the process and the following is a list of symbols suggested by Krystal in her book.

## Protective Symbols

**Balloon or Bubble** - visualised like a soap bubble encompassing rainbow colours and is particularly helpful for someone who is sensitive to even the slightest criticism real or imagined. It is an easy visualisation and good for beginners.

**Plate Glass Screen** - this is a good symbol to visualise when a patient has problems with boss, workmates, in laws etc. It should be visualised as very thick glass, which is shatterproof.

**Cylinder Of Light** - should be used in situations where the client feels very threatened. The cylinder should be energised with specific colours - Krystal suggests gold and also recommends that it should be visualised at night before retiring to sleep and in the mornings but also during the day.

**Pyramid** - although it is an aid to balance it can be used as a visualisation to place oneself within the pyramid and focus on light filling the space within from the top. Some people have found that they are not only more protected but also energised.

**5-Pointed Star** - this works well for various types of psychic attack. The 5 pointed star or pentacle is an old symbol and therefore very powerful as constant use builds up the energy of the symbol. It is suggested that this symbol can be used to protect a house, as well the energy field against negative influences from both spirit and psychic projections. To empower this symbol even more a candle can be burned continuously for several days and Krystal recommends that salt be placed in all four corners of each room whilst a window is left slightly open. Incense can also be burned.

Another use for this symbol is to counteract negative powers used by groups and individuals. In her book Krystal makes the following observation:

"There have been many prophecies and warnings that in the Aquarian Age there will be a confrontation between opposing positive and negative forces, both on the macrocosmic or world scale and on the microcosmic or individual level.

From time to time, we have been asked to help people who have been deluded by an individual or group into believing that they were being introduced to a positive activity or way of life, only to discover later, as they were drawn further into it, that the exact opposite was the case. This often seems to happen to good but naïve people who are unaware that there are negative forces in the world as well as positive ones, and that not everyone has the same motives or beliefs that they have. When such a person realizes what has happened to him, he is usually helplessly under the power of a group or individual and incapable of extricating himself from the situation without help. When we are asked to work on such cases, we are shown protective measures to take to prevent us from being drawn into the same dilemma."

Crystals can be placed at the points to help emphasise the energy of the shape:

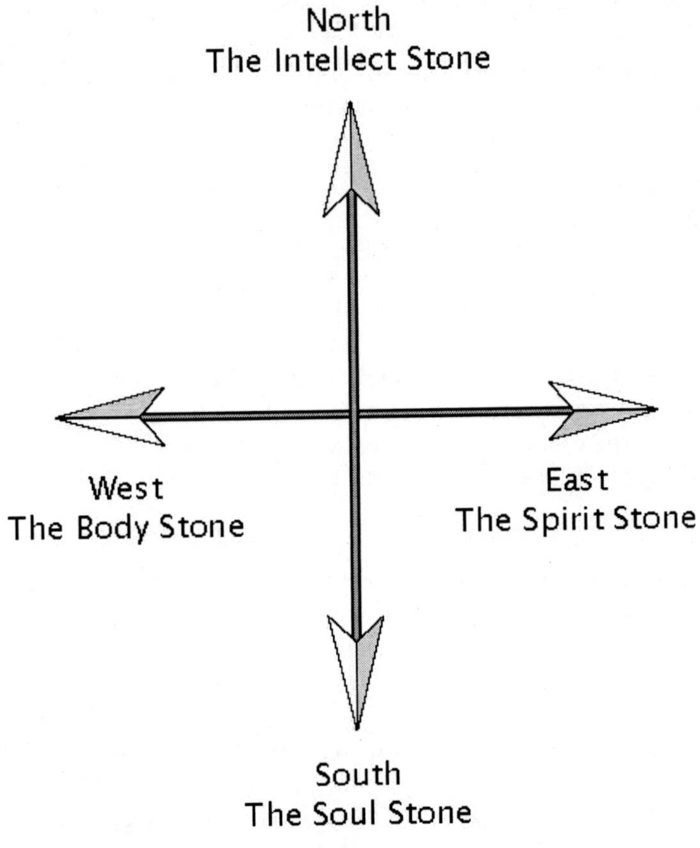

North
The Intellect Stone

West
The Body Stone

East
The Spirit Stone

South
The Soul Stone

DIAGRAM 17 Compass points

In her book Krystal also mentions what she calls the "Inner Enemy" by this she is referring to the aspects within us that prevent us from being the person we wish to be and which works against our best interests. This can take the form of addictions to alcohol or food for example through to an inability to say "no" to people, situations or relationships which are bad for us. Krystal suggests that these "pockets of negativity" which we all have to battle with can be brought over from former incarnations and that we should take care when attempting to release them as they can cause the patient to withdraw from dealing with the pain or fear that can be brought up by becoming seriously ill, developing a dependency on drugs or alcohol, amnesia, insanity or even suicide. If a patient comes to you with a need to release their "Inner Enemy" great care and sensitivity is required in addition to working at the pace that is dictated by the patient. Krystal suggests working with the Figure 8 symbol (see below) and taking time to discuss any experiences, which come up for the patient with them. Be prepared to have to work over a number of sessions to help to clear issues.

## Symbols To Release Faults

**Cosmic Parents** - visualise authority figure(s) that can take away the weakness for you. This may be a way of working with guardian angels or guides.

**A Flame** - visualise a constantly burning flame which can be coloured (violet is said to be the flame of transformation) and into which anything which is wished to be released is thrown and transmuted.

**Figure 8** - Krystal suggest this as a good symbol when working with cutting ties between parents and children but also it is probably one of the best known symbols for tie cutting and can be used for those battling with addictions by placing the addict in one circle and the addiction in the other eg. an alcoholic will visualise a bottle in one circle and him/herself in the other.

This symbol can also be used to cut ties to domination through negative emotions such as fear, guilt, anger, jealousy etc. It is important however, that this practice is carried out on a regular basis.

As the circles separate, it is sometimes necessary to remove the negative through visualisation of burning, burying, or more aggressively destroying with acid or laser beams. Just go with whatever is appropriate for yourself or client. This process can involve a two-visualisation between yourself and your client.

When working with tie cutting, you can incorporate crystals in the following ways:

1. Forming the symbol that you are working with by placing crystals to make the symbol and constructing this around your patient.
2. "Cutting" the ties with a clear quartz crystal wand or termination.
3. Beaming or zapping the tie with crystal energy using a crystal of your choice.

Placing your patient in a protective bubble or balloon which has been enhanced and energised by the addition of a crystal which you have chosen for its protective qualities

## Sacred Geometry and Crystals

Working with sacred geometry can be a very powerful way of harnessing crystal energy. There are a number of geometric archetypes or models which are continually repeated in nature through the petals of flowers, the branches on trees or even the spiral within a sea shell as well as throughout the universe by the spinning galaxies of the cosmos. Sacred geometry was and is still used in the construction of buildings and monuments and by artists when drawing or painting. An experiment in the 1960s carried out by a scientist called Hans Jenny discovered that harmonious sounds when reproduced as form produced patterns and shapes that were symmetrical and geometrically perfect, however, when he used discordant sounds the shapes were corrupted or disfigured.

These sacred shapes are thought to provide a holy blueprint and when formed in crystal grids they can offer a powerful method of realigning and reconnecting the body back into its most appropriate vibrational resonance.

You can place crystals upon these shapes in order to empower still further the energy contained within the diagram, using this method you could either place the grid under a chair or couch and allow the patient to be in the energy of the shape or you could simply meditate upon the pattern you have created. Alternatively, you could easily create the grid by making a pattern of the crystals around the body.

*As always when working with crystals remember to ensure that crystals are cleansed and dedicated before and after working with them.*

THE CIRCLE
Represents the expression of unity, equality and wholeness

THE EGG
Protection and nurturing of the energy field

## THE SQUARE
Symbol of the material world, good for grounding. However, care should be taken when using this symbol that the person receiving the treatment is not stuck in a rut, as this would tend to emphasis this.

## THE EQUIDISTENT CROSS
Represents harmony and balance. It should be placed at the center of the patient or the patient should be sitting in the center of the cross.

## THE CROSS Symbolises protection and perhaps connection with the Christ energy

## THE TRIANGLE
Creates and energizing space

## THE GOLDEN MEAN OR RATIO
This shape represents infinity and our connection to the all that is

## THE FLOWER OF LIFE
This symbol represents the sacred blueprint of all creation

## THE MERKABA
This is considered to be the vehicle, which transports the spirit into different dimensions. MER means LIGHT, KA means SPIRIT and BA means BODY. The Merkaba creates an energy field of light thus separating you from lower vibrations.

It is possible to create a 3 dimensional Merkaba by placing 3 quartz terminations in an inverted triangle with their points facing downwards and forming a Star Of David with the points facing on the subsequent triangle facing upwards. SEE DIAGRAM

DIAGRAM 18 Merkaba

# Working With Angelic Frequencies

Usually, when I am working I call upon the guardian angel of the patient to oversee and help guide what I am doing. I use two pieces of Apophilyte crystals and usually place them either side of the head at about ear level.

It is possible to work with the archetypal energy of Archangels by using crystals that they connect to. Here is a list of Archangels and their energetic frequencies with suggested crystal links:

## MICHAEL
Archangel of the South - FIRE
Encompasses protection, strength, courage, sexual desire, hatred, love, passion, and understanding.
*SUGGESTED APPROPRIATE CRYSTALS: Carnelian, Red and Yellow Jasper.*

## GABRIEL
Archangel of the West - WATER
Encompasses Water, Moon, Goddess, Dreams, Awareness, Gentleness, and Birth.
*SUGGESTED APPROPRIATE CRYSTALS: Aventurine, Aquamarine, and Serpentine*

## RAPHAEL
Archangel, of the East  AIR
Encompasses Teacher, Computer, Creativity, Poetry, Artist, Potter, Healer, and Communication.
*SUGGESTED APPROPRIATE CRYSTALS: Blue Topaz, Chalcedony, Snowy Quartz, And Blue Lance Agate*

## URIEL
Archangel of the North  EARTH
Encompasses Earth, Stones, Devic Kingdoms, Mystery, Darkness

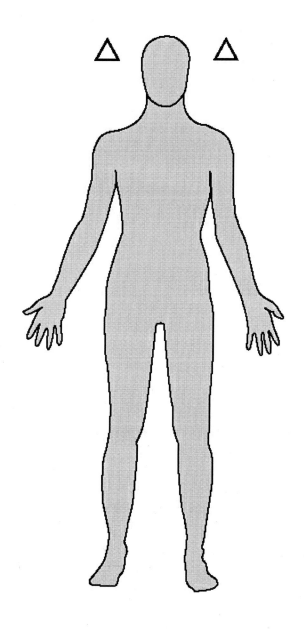

DIAGRAM 19 Body with two Apophylite crystals by the ear

*SUGGESTED APPROPRIATE CRYSTALS: Flint, Agate, and Lodestone*

**AZRAEL**
Archangel of the Center
Encompasses Akashic Records, Spirit, Death and Re-Birth.
*SUGGESTED APPROPRIATE CRYSTALS:*
*Black Tourmaline, Jet, Obsidian, and Apache Tear.*

## WoRking With Wanðs

A wand is a tool which helps to focus your intent and energies. It can be made of a number of materials which can be combined in order to work with different energetic qualities. For instance it can be made of wood either natural or carved with crystals added as embellishments or perhaps a clear quartz termination fixed at the end of the wood which would amplify the energies. Listed below are some commonly used materials in wandmaking:

Copper or copper wire – considered to be an excellent conductor of crystal energies
Crystals – terminations or points, gems or mineral cabochons
Wood
Coloured Beads
Feathers
Leather
Precious metals such as silver and gold

Think of how you feel if someone points at you and you will understand the difference between focussed and unfocussed intent.

Wands have been used throughout history in many and varied cultures. Today we still can see the use of wands in our own society, the Church, the Government and Heads of

State all have access to ceremonial staffs and sceptres which represent the same amplification of energy and are usually made of some of the materials listed above.

## Wooden Wands

When working with wood it is important to note the difference between live wood and dead wood. Live wood is when the tree has given the twig or stick freely. You need to spend some time getting to know the tree and linking into it's vibration so that there is an exchange – after all you need to find out what the qualities are of the wood you plan to use and ask permission from the tree and also that the vibration be retained in the wood you need. Only then should you cut the tree, of course you may find a piece of wood which has fallen from the tree and is still "live". Many people feel that it is important to leave some kind of exchange or it may merely be sufficient to say "thank you". The wood can then be carved or worked in the way that you feel is appropriate.

Users of wooden wands generally find that the energy is gentle and flowing. Green Man Tree Essences (www.greenmanessences.com) have a range of "Wild Woods" which are individually prepared samples of wind-felled British and naturalised woods for use in therapy, attunement and support situations as well as a large range of vibrational tree essences.

## Metal and Crystal Wands

As we have already said crystals can be used to decorate and enhance the energy of wood. However, it is also possible to obtain crystal wands which have been carved – generally most people buy them as usually specialised equipment is needed due to the hardness of the crystal. One notable exception is Selenite which is quite "soft" and easily sanded and fashioned into simple shapes. Great care with it should be taken as it does scratch easily.

Bought wands can be embellished by adding copper or other crystals, feathers, wood etc. Some people work with sacred geometric shapes, usually formed with copper wire which adds another quality again. When wound in a spiral fashion around the wand, the energy is increased and amplified. It is possible to make a very simple wand with a length of copper piping which can the be embellished with crystals and/or wood.

The qualities and energies of a crystal/metal wand is usually much more directional and amplified than a wooden wand

## Using Your Wand

Wands need to be cleansed of negative energies and dedicated to work for the highest good before you use them, the same as you would do with crystals. When using a wand for the first time, it is a good idea to sit and make a connection with it.

Usually it is apparent from the shape and design of the wand, which is the end which will carry and direct the focus of energy and which is the end that will collect or draw the energy into the wand. Spheres are usually used at this end of the wand for this drawing quality.

Generally, the left hand is seen as the receiving hand and the right as the giving hand, therefore most people when using a wand will hold it in their right hand, they may hold it in their left hand to "receive" or tune into the energies of the wand however. It is also down to personal choice of what feels right.

Techniques for cleansing your wand can be as follows, in most cases when clearing the wand the front should be pointed into the earth to allow the energies to flow in that direction in order to be transmuted:

Smudging – using incense, candle smoke, sage to clear the energies
Visualisation – seeing white light flowing through the wand, clearing any negative energies
Blowing down the wand
Intent

## Listed below are some ideas for wand uses:

Drawing symbols
Greater focus of intent
Clearing negative energy – when doing this always ask that the energies being drawn into the wand are transmuted immediately
Connect crystals in a net or grid
Direct energy to a person or place
Clear channels of blocked energies by tracing the directional flow – any blockages will feel "sticky" of sluggish
Creating a circle of protection around a person, place etc.
An aid to meditation
As a "Talking Stick" which can be passed from person to person in much the same way as Native American Indians used the Peace Pipe

# Chapter 8

# Using Crystals With Other Therapies

Crystals lend themselves beautifully to being used in conjunction with other therapies in order to enhance and amplify the overall therapeutic benefits. What follows below are suggested ways in which crystals could be used in different ways in order to combine their energy with the therapy in question but do feel free to be inspired to use crystals in your own way. Experiment and find out what feels right for you.

**Crystals and Reiki**
Reiki is a system of hands on healing which, by a series of attunements, you are able to channel an improved flow of healing energy. It is an excellent method of self-healing, spiritual and personal development. Crystals and Reiki are reputed to have originally come from the same source as Colour and Sound Healing - Atlantis.

The following techniques are suitable only for people who have been attuned to the Reiki 2 level and above as it involves working with the symbols but there is no reason why a Reiki 1 level attunee could not adapt crystals to enhance the energy flow or treatment by working with grounding crystals or by placing crystals within the patients energy field in order to 'fine tune' the healing space.

Programme crystals with Reiki symbols for self healing. Please remember that you will still have to cleanse, dedicate and attune the crystal first though.

Enhancing absent healing techniques - **Working** with two crystals, one which you will keep and the other which should be given to the person who is going to receive absent healing. Attune to the crystals and programme them with the following symbols:

a) *Crystal - 1 Transmitter crystal*: Power symbol, Absent Healing symbol and then the Power symbol again. (This crystal is retained by the Healer).
b) *Crystal - 2 Receiver crystal*: Programme with the absent healing symbol only.

In its simplest form the client can hold the crystal and draw upon the healing energy at either specific times allocated for absent healing or at any given time  whatever is agreed between patient and healer. In addition to this, programming crystals with symbols for clients to use enables them to take responsibility for their own healing by encouraging them to use the crystals in various ways to continue the healing process. This can take the form of using relevant symbols to continue a clearing process or provide added protection etc. It is also ideal for clients who have not received Reiki attunements and therefore do not have knowledge of the symbols.

1. Programme the crystals to hold the energy of the treatment and thereby offer top up sessions that carry the energy of the original treatment without the need to keep visiting the healer.

2. Add power symbols to clear quartz points, wands etc. to increase the effectiveness of the crystals.

3. Add symbols to enhance or amplify gem essences

4. Use crystals to form a grid of a specific Reiki symbol on or around the patient.
5. Add symbols to crystals to enhance connection with another person eg. to promote telepathy, absent healing connections etc.

6. Programme crystals with Reiki symbols to aid grounding or ungrounding

*Using Crystals With Acupuncture and Kinesiology*
Crystal terminations or points can be used to great effect by programming them to remove energy blocks. As with the meridian clearing techniques discussed in Chapter 3, the points can be directed towards the blockage allowing the directional energy of the point to encourage release and energise energy flow.

By reversing the point it is also possible to release over energy but this should be done with great care and awareness.

Again, always ensure that crystals are cleansed and dedicated effectively before and after using them.

## Using Crystals Facials and Body Treatments

Using crystals when giving a facial can be a great enhancement to the experience. Crystals can be used to set the space and to help relax, de-stress etc. by using the pyramid technique in the book or by simply placing a crystal under the couch or chair. As well as this you can use a crystal 'wand' to work on pressure points around the face, neck and body.

See also below in the aromatherapy section, techniques for combining oils with crystals which can be used also to energise face creams, skin toners, etc.

## Using Crystals For Reflexology

Reflexology points upon the body can be stimulated or calmed down by the use of specifically chosen crystals. Simply select a crystal and hold the crystal near the reflex point, which you wish to work on. You may wish to add some pressure or alternatively, if you have a very sensitive patient you may find that as you work off of the body they are able to respond and feel energy shifting.

## Using Crystals For Hypnotherapy, Counseling and Psychotherapy

Programming and attuning a crystal for your client to hold during sessions may aid the release process. You can also use crystals to create an appropriate atmosphere in the room and to dispel any negativity that may be released.

*Using Crystals With Astrology*
At a very basic level, crystals can be related to birth dates. Thus the following crystals relate to the signs of the zodiac:

21 December 19 January
CAPRICORN: Turquoise, Jet, Black Onyx, Clear Quartz, Black Tourmaline.

20 January 18 February
AQUARIUS: Garnet, Turquoise, Amethyst, Onyx, Ruby, Diamond, Jade, and Sapphire.

19 February  20 April
PISCES : Amethyst, Turquoise, Pearl, Rose Quartz, Calcite, Aquamarine, Bloodstone.

21 March  20 April
ARIES: Bloodstone, Carnelian, Jasper, Diamond, Aquamarine, Emerald, Ruby, Coral, and Hematite.

21 April  20 May
TAURUS: Rose Quartz, Emerald, Diamond, Tourmaline, Tigers Eye, Topaz, Lapis Lazuli.

21 May  20 June
GEMINI : Moonstone, Agate, Emerald, Aquamarine, Calcite.

21 June  21 August
CANCER: Emerald, Chrysoprase, Pearl, Ruby, Moonstone, Amber.

21 July  21 August
LEO:  Clear Quartz, Onyx, Turquoise, Ruby, Topaz, Sunstone, and Emerald.

22 August  22 September
VIRGO:  Carnelian, Moonstone, Sapphire, Opal, Peridot, Sodalite, Rutile Quartz.

23 September  22 October
LIBRA: Peridot, Topaz, Opal, Lapis Lazuli, Aventurine, Emerald, Jade.

23 October  22 November
SCORPIO:  Aquamarine, Dark Opal, Turquoise, Obsidian, Smoky Quartz, Herkimer Diamond.

23 November  22 December

SAGITTARIUS: Topaz, Amethyst, Malachite, Blue Lace Agate, Flint, Turquoise.

It is important, however, to go by your intuitive selection and get a crystal because you are drawn to it rather than buying a crystal which is said to relate to your birthdate. You may find that from the list you can see some that you like or resonate with and some that do not appeal to you at all.

Crystals can also be placed onto birth charts to heal or energise aspects of the chart or zodiac sign.

## Using Crystals With Aromatherapy

Crystals can be used to energise aromatherapy oils and other lotions and positions. This process can be carried out in many different ways.

a) If you make a gem essence, add drops to the other ingredients eg. when preparing a massage oil or skin toner etc.

b) Energise oils by simply placing the oil on top or close to a crystal

c) Energise oils by using a visualization technique. Holding the crystal you wish to energise the oil with in your left hand and a quartz point or termination in your right, pointing the termination at the bottle you wish to energise. Close your eyes and visualize the energy from the crystal in your left hand, flowing up your left arm and into the heart Chakra. Then see the energy continuing to the right arm and down into the quartz point where it is magnified and transferred to the bottle of oil. Particularly good combinations are Rose Quartz and Rose or Lavender and Amethyst.

Obviously you can set the space in much the same way as with facials and other treatments.

## Using Crystals With Homeopathy

It is possible to make homeopathic remedies of crystals and this is being done currently by a homeopathic pharmacy called Helios who are based in Tunbridge Wells. The remedies can be made by adding drops of gem elixirs to the pills and then the usual succussion techniques carried out.

It is also possible for other remedies to be energized by placing on a clear quartz cluster.

## Using Crystals With Colour Therapy

As has already been mentioned in a previous chapter, it is possible to link different coloured crystals in order to create a Chakra set to enable the healer to energise chakras by working with the therapeutic effects of colour. It is also possible to link this in with the emotional aspects of colour for example, carrying a green coloured stone may promote a sense of calmness and tranquility whilst red may provide an energy boost.

In addition to this some colour and crystal healers are aware of the effect of incorporating light. It is possible to buy light boxes which can greatly enhance the appearance of some crystals (Selenite, calcite and quartz respond to light particularly well) for display purposes but the light boxes also have an energetic impact, which I feel heightens the qualities already present within the crystals.

Some colour therapists work with a torch, which has a crystal point, connected to it. The beam from the torch is then transmitted through the crystal termination that is directed at acupuncture points on the body in order to remove blockages. These torches usually come with a clear quartz crystal point and a selection of coloured filters, which can be selected, as appropriate.

## Using Crystals With Affirmations To Enhance Willpower and Positive Thought.

Using crystals to empower affirmations by programming the crystal to hold the energetic imprint of the affirmation and to magnify the intent behind it.

The crystal could then be held during meditation, at times of crisis or lack of willpower.

Clear quartz would be a particularly relevant crystal for this.

## Using Crystals With Feng Shui

Crystals can be used to enhance and tailor the flow and qualities of chi energy. A clear quartz cluster will promote harmony and balance within a room, whilst a rose quartz chunk will emit a loving and nurturing energy into a room. You can hang quartz in windows rather than the faceted lead crystals more commonly used to retain the chi within the home. A crystal carved into Feng Shui symbols such as dragons etc will further enhance their effects.

# Chapter 9

# Earth Energies

On one level, Feng Shui has raised an awareness of how energy other than our own can affect us. Most of us would agree that when we have tidied up a room, it can make us feel better within ourselves, conversely when we are in a cluttered environment we feel confused and our energy is diminished. Many of us experience a sense of release when we clear out wardrobes, cupboards etc. In its simplest form space clearing can be energizing and improve the atmosphere within our homes and workplace. A positive step towards creating the correct atmosphere to amplify any healing given or received.

Stagnant energy can also be caused by illness, friction, bad news, electromagnetic fields sometimes known as geopathic stress which are enhanced by the ever-increasing list of electrical items, which we accumulate in the home.

There are many ways of clearing 'stuck' energy from smudging (burning incense or a sage stick) within a room to clapping hands, ringing bells or even banging drums in areas where stagnant energy is detected.

A quick and simple form of space clearing that I use from time to time is to place each of the following items in a corner of the room: a lit candle, a bowl of salt, a bowl of water and burning incense or a suitably cleansing oil such as sage or rosemary. Once the candle and the incense or oil have finished burning remove the items and throw them all away.
It is possible to make your own smudge stick from any

combination of herbs that you may have growing in your garden. Just tie them tightly in a bundle and place in the airing cupboard until they are quite dry. Then light and use as you wish.

TVs, microwave cookers, mobile telephones, computers etc, substantially increase electromagnetic stress. These can be alleviated by the use of Rose Quartz crystals as we have already discussed in previous chapters. The natural energy lines, which we find, can be negative to our well being such as water lines.

If we take a macrocosmic/microcosmic view of the world and its interconnectedness to us we become aware that we are as responsible for the earth as we are for ourselves. The only difference is that the Earth could probably live very well without us whilst the opposite is not true for humanity.

Many people, as they acquire an awareness of how the Earth sustains us, begin to feel drawn to work on healing the Earth.

Some psychics claimed that the earth has chakras, which are often thought to be on sacred sites all over the earth, just like we do. As we begin to develop an understanding of leylines we can see that possibly there is a similarity between these leylines and the meridians that we have within our own physical bodies.

But what are leylines? It was only 80 years ago that leylines were discovered (or should it be rediscovered?) by Alfred Watkins. His book entitled *The Old Straight Track* which was published in 1925 is still in print. He discovered when looking at a map one day that many ancient and sacred sites such as churches but also places that were sacred to old pagan religions, were aligned in a straight line. He chose to call them leys as he found that the local place names provided evidence that this is what they had once been called. He described the experience he had of connecting this knowledge together as if a 'flood of ancestral memory' had entered his consciousness.

An example of a lay line is the Gloucestershire Saintbury Ley that was discovered by Paul Devereux and Ian Thomas. It is about three and a half miles or 5.6 kilometers in length. It runs in a straight line from the Vale of Evesham, via the village of Saintbury and through to the Cotswolds. This line encompasses points such as a crossroads which has a wayside cross, Saintbury Church within which there is an altar which pre-dates Christianity, a round barrow which is dated as Bronze Age, a Neolithic long barrow which is sited in the middle of an Iron Age Fort and a Saxon pagan cemetery. The leyline comes to an end at Seven Wells Farm, which is very ancient and is surrounded by a semi-circle of trees and was the setting, which inspired a novel by Hugh Ross Williamson, called *The Silver Bowl* which depicted the continued existence of witchcraft within the area.

Other civilizations have discovered these energy lines for example, the Chinese talk of dragon lines which they acknowledge within the concepts of Feng Shui and in Peru there are the famous Naxca lines which are drawn out apparently randomly but when viewed from the sky (something the ancients would not have been able to do) show depictions of animals and other geometric shapes, spirals and lines, some over 6 miles long. These lines had to be scraped from the desert surface and why all this work was carried out when the only view possible was from the air remains shrouded in mystery.

It is possible to dowse for leylines either present on site or by using a map.

Crystals can be placed on the map or at the site. Great care should be taken to ensure that the work is appropriate for the

Earth. Any work you carry out should always be dedicated to the highest good and the harm of none so that anything that is inappropriate is negated. Too many people, armed with the resurgence of this knowledge, are affecting and diverting the energetic flow of leylines and this can sometimes be inappropriate and therefore not particularly positive.

Newspapers and magazines are more and more documenting Geopathic and environmental stress. The increasing use of microwaves, mobile telephones (and their masts), the widespread use of computers both in the office as well as in the home, the effects of increasing deforestations, genetically modified farming, irradiated food to name but a few, are increasingly having an impact on us and our world around us.

Crystals can help but ultimately unless we take steps to change the way that we live and travel we will continue to adversely affect the food chain and the earths delicate ecological balance. This urgently needs to be addressed both individually and globally. Hopefully, the spiritual and personal development that is stimulated by crystal (and other vibrational therapies) will encourage everyone to take a more responsible and less selfish stance in changing attitudes and behaviour which will benefit the earth to a greater degree other than simply placing crystals in order to alleviate rather than remove the negative impact of geopathic or environmental stress.

# Chapter 10

# Historical References To Crystals

## Atlantis - Did It Exist?

Many clairvoyants, most famously Edgar Cayce, claim Atlantis really existed, that it's empire embraced parts of America-Africa-Europe and Asia. In a single day and night some 10,000 years ago it is said that Atlantis was destroyed by flood and earthquake. Legend has it that abuse by it's people of crystal based technology led to the disaster but that survivors of Atlantis fled to other civilizations all over the world such as the Mayans, Native American Indians for example and passed on some of their knowledge to these people.

Atlanteans were said to be one of the first purely spiritual races on Earth - they gradually lost this over many generations in their quest to understand wisdom and knowledge. Prior to Atlantis, God is said to have attempted to create physical reality with Lemuria or Mu. Archangels laid down Leylines and taught Muons how to live. They were non-physical beings living in a glorious land of milk and honey, although they lived on prana. They were balanced and androgynous and lived forever. After some time, God decided that this was not working and sent Azrael to wipe them out. Azrael was ordered to divide up the lands. He called in Sanat Kumara, the earth's consciousness and Gaia, the earth's spirit and they drew up plans. They decided to create Atlantis to hold God's spiritual race, the other continents would hold different races with different traits.

Seven skulls were reputed to have been given to the Atlanteans by God. These skulls were used to magnify the energy of crystals, to bring into manifestation anything, which was required, and to enable miracles to be performed. When Atlantis was completed the skulls were placed in the Primary Temple that was made of pure crystal and situated in the main City area. The Temple passed the laws for the entire continent and the Kings. In the beginning, priests asked the skulls for advice and healing from God. People initially didn't get ill; the only injuries were from accidents. The Temples didn't have stairs; they were accessed by levitation only. Atlanteans who were unable to levitate did not gain access to the Temples and were thought of as being physically handicapped. These people became regarded as the lower race of the society and lived in farming communities by the sea. After some time these communities came to worship Poseidon.

Initially, Atlantis was based on equality. All the people were telepathic, psychic, able to levitate, manifest etc. They used "tools" such as meditation, aromatherapy, and colour and lived purely on pranic or life force energy rather than food. As all Atlanteans were telepathic there was very little opportunity to rebel as everybody could read each others thoughts! However, over a period of time, some Atlanteans began to disagree with the farming communities being treated as outcasts and these people went to live in the hills. They became a separate society and were known as "The Inspirers". Some Atlanteans went to live underground. Subterranean Atlantis had huge cave like structures and beautiful crystal caves.

Atlanteans' life expectancy was between 2 and 3 hundred years. If a soul wanted to incarnate, a priest would be contacted to aid the process. The soul would choose the parents; sex would take place purely in order to facilitate the incarnation (children incarnated due to any deviation from this process were deemed in much the same way as illegitimate children were/are in our society). Priestesses brought up children, not the biological parents who separated once they had carried out the roles assigned to them.

Likewise, when a soul felt that they had achieved all that they could they would initiate their own physical death.

As generations passed, people forgot what the skulls were for. Fourteen smaller skulls were made to connect with the seven larger ones. People began to lose touch with the Angels and with God. They began to trade worldwide and went to war with Greece.

The Atlanteans were believed to have had contact with extra-terrestrials. Primarily Sirius the Dog star which is the brightest in the universe. They are reputed to have taught the Atlanteans dimensional travel, time travel, sacred geometry, laser technology, maths, genetic engineering, cloning, dimensional doorways and encouraged the Atlanteans to questions themselves and God.

The Atlanteans began to experiment with genetics and constructed a slave race which were half animals-half man. They planted crystals and symbols in heads and the spine areas to control people who did not toe the line. Some people believe that these "implants" still lie within the energy pattern today of the bodies of those people who received these processes, and are becoming evident now as they need to be removed.

At this time the Atlanteans disturbed the balance of nature by creating synthetic herbs, they built a central tower to challenge the natural authority of God. It is thought that the "Tower of Babel" mentioned in the Bible refers to this tower - "God smote them down, after the tower collapsed they all spoke different languages". Some Atlanteans were pre-warned and fled before it's downfall to Egypt, Inca, Maya, America where some of the Atlantean knowledge was retained such as use of crystals, skulls etc.

It has been put forward that Hitler tried to recreate Atlantis. He believed that if he could bring back the Arian race, then he could recapture Atlantis's magic. Himmler was the main supporter of this, he believed that the remaining Atlanteans had moved to Europe and were a Nordic race. The racial qualities were that everyone had to be 5'9" or above with blonde hair, blue eyes, lineage back to 1750 with no outside marriages.

## Plato's Atlantis (427-347 BC)

Great, great grandson of Solon, the philosopher Plato taught immortality and reincarnation. He said "There have been and will be many different calamities to destroy mankind, the greatest by fire and water. From an island larger that Libya and Asia combined that lay opposite the strait you call 'Pillars of Hercules', a great empire had invaded Europe to be defeated by Ancient Greeks. Later in a single dreadful day and night, earthquake and flood swallowed Greek armies and Atlantis was swallowed by sea and vanished".

Plato records that 10 Kings ruled Atlantis each ruling over their own territory. They adhered to the laws, which were engraved upon the Temple of Poseidon.

Whether all of this stretches the bounds of your personal belief system or not, one thing that is certain is that crystals have been and are still used in many different cultures and civilizations. For example the Native American Indians medicine men worked with crystals (primarily Turquoise) for healing and sacred rituals, they believe that there is a crystal matrix (which science now appears to be in the process of confirming to be true) and that crystals can help us to access different dimensions of understanding and reality.

This belief of connecting with different dimensions and realities can be seen again and again throughout ancient civilizations which although not geographically linked, still seem to form a consensus of opinion.

In recent times there has been a resurgence of interest in crystal skulls. The most well known of which is the Mitchell-Hedges skull which was found in a Mayan temple in British Honduras in 1924 by the Anna Mitchell-Hedges, the daughter of an archeologist. This interest in crystal skulls has been well documented in the book *The Mystery Of The Crystal Skulls* by Chris Morton and Ceri Thomas.

In, what we like to think of as our more civilized western world, there is still a great emphasis that is placed upon crystals, which even today are still seen as symbols of power, beauty and wealth. Whilst the conventional church and its religious authorities may not acknowledge their healing and spiritual properties, they still use crystals in articles connected with ritual and ceremony such as the jewel encrusted sceptres and crosses. Our own royal family own a tremendous amount of jewellery, eclipsed somewhat by the Crown Jewels, which are surrounded by myth and legends in themselves.

Perhaps our modern western civilization is not so very far removed from the shamans and witch doctors of less evolved communities.

# Chapter 11

# Working Professionally

If you wish to work with crystals on a professional basis it is important to get a recognized qualification. The Affiliation of Crystal Healing Organizations (their address is in the back of the book) is an association whose members adhere to a set standard of teaching and their courses are validated by the Open College Network. The courses for professional qualification are run over a 2-year period and students are taught an agreed core curriculum. Completion of this course enables students to obtain insurance in order to practice and goes some way towards encouraging the mainstream acceptance of crystal therapy.

Starting up a practice can be hard. You need to be a jack-of-all-trades as well as a master of crystals! The following points are things that need to be considered if you are thinking of working with any therapy professionally:

PRACTICE MANAGEMENT

## 1. Initial Considerations
When you decide that you would like to start a professional practice it is important to consider initially to understand that being self employed is not easy and takes a great deal of determination and motivation. One has to be able to do the job effectively but also to be extremely self motivated and have the ability to go out encourage people to come to you.

You need to be able to think creatively in order to bring your therapy to the notice of potential customers. In addition to this, if you have never been self employed before, you need to be aware of the different pressures that come with the territory fluctuating income, need to keep adequate financial records, sometimes lack of support and companionship that you get when working with other people in the same environment etc.

In addition to this it is vitally important that you ensure that your motivation is sound, that you are as clear as possible energetically and that this optimum energetic state is maintained vigorously.

## 2. Life Planning

It is no good giving up a well-paid job if you have high financial outgoings, such as a mortgage to consider without putting alternative financial arrangements in place. Strategically plan how you are going to receive financial recompense. It may be easier to continue in paid employment, endeavoring to reduce the financial load whilst working at building up your practice in your spare time. Alternatively you may be able to cut down the amount of hours you spend in paid employment in order to begin to start your practice. Set realistic targets for you to achieve and follow them through.

## 3. Success Strategies

As we have said, in order to get things off the ground, it is helpful if you begin to set goals for yourself to achieve. Do you want to work in a clinic? If so set yourself a target of telephoning or writing to 6 therapy centers in your area. Be disciplined about your targets.

Look at how you manage your time and try to make it more effective. If you are treating friends ask them to recommend you to others.

Keep a clear balance in your life between work and relaxation. It is important that you ensure that you practice what you preach and do not get caught up in the trap of living purely to work.

## 4. Conscious Business

Be aware of behaving in a professional manner. Ensure that you have adequate insurance and that you have the appropriate equipment that a patient would expect from you for example a couch and a reasonable space to work in. If you are working from home try to have a room, which is used solely for this purpose, if this is not possible, ensure that the room is tidy and clean.

Assess the image and the ethics of what you are doing. If you have clients who are able to pay you a reasonable sum of money for treatments why not give free treatments to others who are not so financially well off. I feel strongly that therapies are not available to all due to the high cost of training, insurance, premises etc. Rather than get into a situation where I am virtually means testing my clients I choose to work with support groups where I can connect and give freely. If I do a free treatment for a friend, I personally feel that there is a need for an energetic exchange. That is to say that I would swap therapies with them or they will provide me with something else other than money. This can be as simple as a bunch of flowers but I feel that it is important that you do not allow others to take your time and efforts for granted. It also ensures that there is a value placed upon the work that you have done and this hopefully means that they will have a commitment to work with any issues that come up for them in order to aid the healing processes.

## 5. Business Start Up

As discussed above, you need to ensure that you have adequate insurance cover. It is as well to think long and hard about you wish to work. Do you want to work from home or from a therapy center or perhaps from both? You need to work out an appropriate fee structure. Working from home should not be as expensive as working from a therapy center where you can expect to pay a quarter to a third of the fee to them for the use of their facilities and room.

Take into account factors such as location, a business name, financing and research the area you choose to work in thoroughly. It will be harder for your to set up if there are a number of other therapists offering similar services to yourself in the same area.

## 6. Business Management

When setting up choose your advisors carefully. For example, when selecting an accountant, pick someone who is sympathetic to your therapy and services. Ensure that you are fully aware of all fees that you will be asked to pay, in some therapy centers although they expect you to pay for room hire, at certain other times in the year there is another charge for advertising which is sometimes passed onto the therapists in the practice. Make yourself aware of policies and procedures that are in place wherever you work so that you dont inadvertently step on someones toes.

## 7. Financial Management

Always ensure that you keep your bookkeeping up to date and in order. It will be far more stressful and expensive if you allow them to become incomplete and confused. Be prepared for and set aside a realistic amount of money for any taxes which will become due.

## 8. Communications

Communicate effectively what you are offering. This can be by asking (and sometimes offering an incentive such as a free treatment) existing clients to recommend you to others, by placing advertising in local papers or magazines, Thomson local or Yellow Pages, leaving leaflets in shops, libraries, local office information boards etc giving information about what you offer.

Building professional reciprocal alliances with other therapists and practitioners offering therapies which are complementary to yours in order that you can refer on to others, patients who need another type of therapy and vice versa.

## 9. Marketing

When looking at the marketing of your therapy services there are a number of things that you can use: Advertising, build your own website and regularly update it, target markets and assess how best to gain a foothold within these markets would it be by telephoning them, e-mailing or sending information through the post for example or simply by offering to do an introductory talk? Ensure that your leaflets and business cards are well presented. If necessary, employ a graphic artist or someone who is proficient on one of the publishing programmes available on your computer. Think about who you want your client base to be  do you want to offer your services to women only for example?

## 10. The Business Plan

Most businesses (for that is what you are aiming to be) have a Business Plan. This is something which you can do very easily. Simply put down on paper a vision of what you would like to have achieved within say a 5 year time span and then think of ways that you will be able to achieve this vision. Refer and update this plan frequently in order to help you to keep your focus on where you are going and to motivate you when things seem to be hard.

If you need to get finance from a bank you are often asked to provide them with a Business Plan before they will even consider lending you any money.

Finally, try to work with an understanding of universal law. In business we try to gain work in any way that is appropriate. When carrying out spiritual work we accept that in theory there should be an exchange of energy and that we will receive the clients who we need to work with. There is no need to behave in an aggressive or selfish way when working. You will find that if you behave with the utmost integrity it always pays dividends.

# Final Conclusion

The reawakening awareness of Crystals and their therapeutic properties have, along with an increase in knowledge regarding other spiritual truths, led to an increasing interest in magic in all senses of the word. What we can achieve, in some cases, with the aid of crystals and this knowledge can be truly miraculous. However, my concern is that the ability to manifest can be abused and I would urge everyone working with crystals to ensure that they are working from a point of neutrality. That is to say that they are committed to allow the Universe, God or whatever their truth is to determine the ultimate outcome of any work carried out. It is not for us to manipulate our relationships, illnesses, material circumstances etc. but to allow any necessary processes to unfold in order that the appropriate karmic, spiritual or personal lessons are taken on board and resolved rather than postponed for another day or even lifetime.

Crystal therapy plays a part in spiritual and personal development by highlighting lessons to be learned, giving us the necessary energetic 'push' and support to enable us to resolve and/or understand difficult situations and circumstances which we find ourselves experiencing. They are not there to prevent these processes from unfolding but merely to ease or quicken the pace of the process.

Wherever possible try to ensure that you are working from the heart rather than the ego. Do not ask for a specific outcome but rather ask your guides or helpers to direct the energy appropriately. This can be difficult as we all need some kind of reassurance but, I believe, that ultimately this approach will lead to the best possible conclusion to difficult circumstances which we all encounter during our lives in order to allow the souls ultimate growth and development to take place.

In working with crystals you will encounter great wonder and even joy. I wish you all that and more in your journey through life.

Shirley O'Donoghue June 2001

# Appendix

# Healing Grids or Placements

Crystals should be placed around the patient's body which should be either lying down as shown in the illustrations or sitting in a chair.

The shape should then be drawn in with a wand by tracing the shape with the wand or joining up the one dimensional gaps. You will find that the shape will form as a three dimensional shape once the wand has been used. Use your hands and/or a pendulum to check the changes in the energy surrounding the patient. It is advisable to only stay in the grid for a maximum of around 15 minutes per session or less. For those less experienced 5 minutes would probably be sufficient.

These grids are based on sacred geometry which acknowledges the energy of shape and form. The shapes incorporated into these grids are known as the Platonic Solids which are considered to be natures building blocks. They are ancient and can be traced back as far as the Pythagorean Mystery School in Ancient Greece and are still used by mathematicians and scientists, in more recent times we are finding links with these shapes in DNA and crystalline structures.

## Grid 1 Cube or Hexahedron

Element – Earth
Direction - North
State – Solid
Crystals – Use 4 Pyrite or Fool's Gold
Key words – Grounding and Centring

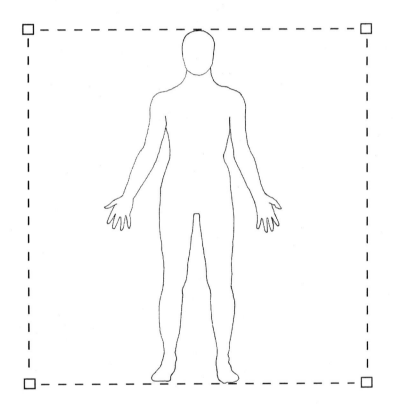

**Grid 2 Icosahedrons**
Element – Water
Direction - West
State – Liquid
Crystals – Use Blue Calcite
Key words – Transformation and release

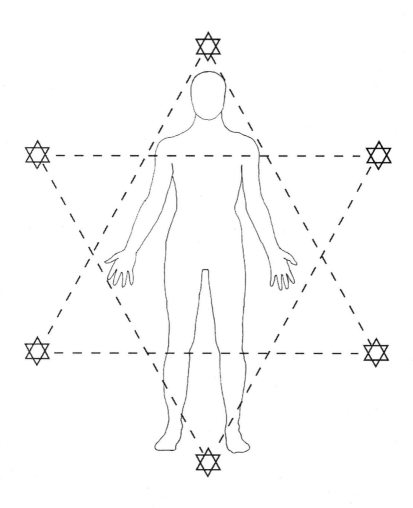

## Grid 3 Octahedron
Element – Air
Direction - East
State – Gas
Crystals – Use Clear Quartz
Key words – Protection and transmutation

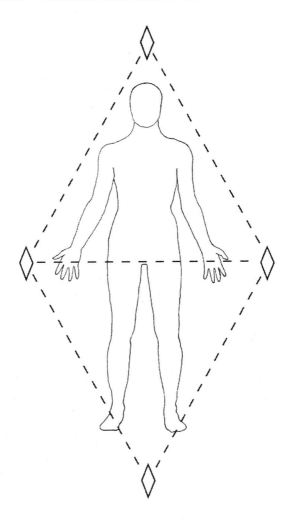

**Grid 4 Tetrahedron**
Element – Fire
Direction - South
State – Heat
Crystals –  Use Carnelian
Key words – Inner guidance

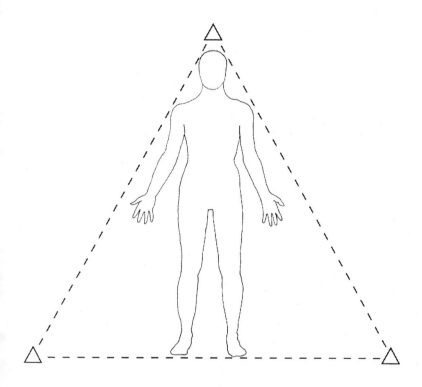

# Grid 5 Dodecahedron

Element – Universe
Direction - Centre
State – Ether
Crystals – Amethyst
Key words – Balance, equilibrium and deep healing

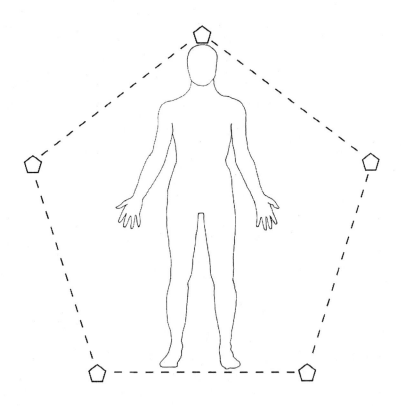

# FREE DETAILED CATALOGUE

Capall Bann is owned and run by people actively involved in many of the areas in which we publish. A detailed illustrated catalogue is available on request, SAE or International Postal Coupon appreciated. **Titles can be ordered direct from Capall Bann, post free in the UK** (cheque or PO with order) or from good bookshops and specialist outlets.

Do contact us for details on the latest releases at: **Capall Bann Publishing, Auton Farm, Milverton, Somerset, TA4 1NE.** Titles include:

A Breath Behind Time, Terri Hector
Angels and Goddesses - Celtic Christianity & Paganism, M. Howard
Arthur - The Legend Unveiled, C Johnson & E Lung
Astrology The Inner Eye - A Guide in Everyday Language, E Smith
Auguries and Omens - The Magical Lore of Birds, Yvonne Aburrow
Asyniur - Womens Mysteries in the Northern Tradition, S McGrath
Beginnings - Geomancy, Builder's Rites & Electional Astrology in the
      European Tradition, Nigel Pennick
Between Earth and Sky, Julia Day
Book of the Veil , Peter Paddon
Caer Sidhe - Celtic Astrology and Astronomy, Vol 1, Michael Bayley
Caer Sidhe - Celtic Astrology and Astronomy, Vol 2 M Bayley
Call of the Horned Piper, Nigel Jackson
Cat's Company, Ann Walker
Celtic Faery Shamanism, Catrin James
Celtic Faery Shamanism - The Wisdom of the Otherworld, Catrin James
Celtic Lore & Druidic Ritual, Rhiannon Ryall
Celtic Sacrifice - Pre Christian Ritual & Religion, Marion Pearce
Celtic Saints and the Glastonbury Zodiac, Mary Caine
Circle and the Square, Jack Gale
Compleat Vampyre - The Vampyre Shaman, Nigel Jackson
Creating Form From the Mist - The Wisdom of Women in Celtic Myth and
      Culture, Lynne Sinclair-Wood
Crystal Clear - A Guide to Quartz Crystal, Jennifer Dent
Crystal Doorways, Simon & Sue Lilly
Crystals Healing and Folklore, David Rankine
Crossing the Borderlines - Guising, Masking & Ritual Animal Disguise in the
      European Tradition, Nigel Pennick
Dragons of the West, Nigel Pennick
Earth Dance - A Year of Pagan Rituals, Jan Brodie
Earth Harmony - Places of Power, Holiness & Healing, Nigel Pennick

Earth Magic, Margaret McArthur

Eildon Tree (The) Romany Language & Lore, Michael Hoadley

Enchanted Forest - The Magical Lore of Trees, Yvonne Aburrow

Eternal Priestess, Sage Weston

Eternally Yours Faithfully, Roy Radford & Evelyn Gregory

Everything You Always Wanted To Know About Your Body, But So Far
    Nobody's Been Able To Tell You, Chris Thomas & D Baker

Face of the Deep - Healing Body & Soul, Penny Allen

Fairies in the Irish Tradition, Molly Gowen

Familiars - Animal Powers of Britain, Anna Franklin

Fool's First Steps, (The) Chris Thomas

Forest Paths - Tree Divination, Brian Harrison, Ill. S. Rouse

From Past to Future Life, Dr Roger Webber

Gardening For Wildlife Ron Wilson

God Year, The, Nigel Pennick & Helen Field

Goddess on the Cross, Dr George Young

Goddess Year, The, Nigel Pennick & Helen Field

Goddesses, Guardians & Groves, Jack Gale

Handbook For Pagan Healers, Liz Joan

Handbook of Fairies, Ronan Coghlan

Healing Book, The, Chris Thomas and Diane Baker

Healing Homes, Jennifer Dent

Healing Journeys, Paul Williamson

Healing Stones, Sue Philips

Herb Craft - Shamanic & Ritual Use of Herbs, Lavender & Franklin

Hidden Heritage - Exploring Ancient Essex, Terry Johnson

Hub of the Wheel, Skytoucher

In Search of Herne the Hunter, Eric Fitch

Inner Celtia, Alan Richardson & David Annwn

Inner Mysteries of the Goths, Nigel Pennick

Inner Space Workbook - Develop Thru Tarot, C Summers & J Vayne

Intuitive Journey, Ann Walker Isis - African Queen, Akkadia Ford

Journey Home, The, Chris Thomas

Kecks, Keddles & Kesh - Celtic Lang & The Cog Almanac, Bayley

Language of the Psycards, Berenice

Legend of Robin Hood, The, Richard Rutherford-Moore

Lid Off the Cauldron, Patricia Crowther

Light From the Shadows - Modern Traditional Witchcraft, Gwyn

Living Tarot, Ann Walker

Lore of the Sacred Horse, Marion Davies

Lost Lands & Sunken Cities (2nd ed.), Nigel Pennick

Magic of Herbs - A Complete Home Herbal, Rhiannon Ryall

Magical Guardians - Exploring the Spirit and Nature of Trees, Philip Heselton

Magical History of the Horse, Janet Farrar & Virginia Russell

Magical Lore of Animals, Yvonne Aburrow

Magical Lore of Cats, Marion Davies

**176**

Magical Lore of Herbs, Marion Davies
Magick Without Peers, Ariadne Rainbird & David Rankine
Masks of Misrule - Horned God & His Cult in Europe, Nigel Jackson
Medicine For The Coming Age, Lisa Sand MD
Medium Rare - Reminiscences of a Clairvoyant, Muriel Renard
Menopausal Woman on the Run, Jaki da Costa
Mind Massage - 60 Creative Visualisations, Marlene Maundrill
Mirrors of Magic - Evoking the Spirit of the Dewponds, P Heselton
Moon Mysteries, Jan Brodie
Mysteries of the Runes, Michael Howard
Mystic Life of Animals, Ann Walker
New Celtic Oracle The, Nigel Pennick & Nigel Jackson
Oracle of Geomancy, Nigel Pennick
Pagan Feasts - Seasonal Food for the 8 Festivals, Franklin & Phillips
Patchwork of Magic - Living in a Pagan World, Julia Day
Pathworking - A Practical Book of Guided Meditations, Pete Jennings
Personal Power, Anna Franklin
Pickingill Papers - The Origins of Gardnerian Wicca, Bill Liddell
Pillars of Tubal Cain, Nigel Jackson
Places of Pilgrimage and Healing, Adrian Cooper
Practical Divining, Richard Foord
Practical Meditation, Steve Hounsome
Practical Spirituality, Steve Hounsome
Psychic Self Defence - Real Solutions, Jan Brodie
Real Fairies, David Tame
Reality - How It Works & Why It Mostly Doesn't, Rik Dent
Romany Tapestry, Michael Houghton
Runic Astrology, Nigel Pennick
Sacred Animals, Gordon MacLellan
Sacred Celtic Animals, Marion Davies, Ill. Simon Rouse
Sacred Dorset - On the Path of the Dragon, Peter Knight
Sacred Grove - The Mysteries of the Forest, Yvonne Aburrow
Sacred Geometry, Nigel Pennick
Sacred Nature, Ancient Wisdom & Modern Meanings, A Cooper
Sacred Ring - Pagan Origins of British Folk Festivals, M. Howard
Season of Sorcery - On Becoming a Wisewoman, Poppy Palin
Seasonal Magic - Diary of a Village Witch, Paddy Slade
Secret Places of the Goddess, Philip Heselton
Secret Signs & Sigils, Nigel Pennick
Self Enlightenment, Mayan O'Brien
Spirits of the Air, Jaq D Hawkins
Spirits of the Earth, Jaq D Hawkins
Spirits of the Earth, Jaq D Hawkins
Stony Gaze, Investigating Celtic Heads John Billingsley
Stumbling Through the Undergrowth , Mark Kirwan-Heyhoe
Subterranean Kingdom, The, revised 2nd ed, Nigel Pennick

Symbols of Ancient Gods, Rhiannon Ryall
Talking to the Earth, Gordon MacLellan
Taming the Wolf - Full Moon Meditations, Steve Hounsome
Teachings of the Wisewomen, Rhiannon Ryall
The Other Kingdoms Speak, Helena Hawley
Tree: Essence of Healing, Simon & Sue Lilly
Tree: Essence, Spirit & Teacher, Simon & Sue Lilly
Through the Veil, Peter Paddon
Torch and the Spear, Patrick Regan
Understanding Chaos Magic, Jaq D Hawkins
Vortex - The End of History, Mary Russell
Warp and Weft - In Search of the I-Ching, William de Fancourt
Warriors at the Edge of Time, Jan Fry
Water Witches, Tony Steele
Way of the Magus, Michael Howard
Weaving a Web of Magic, Rhiannon Ryall
West Country Wicca, Rhiannon Ryall
Wildwitch - The Craft of the Natural Psychic, Poppy Palin
Wildwood King , Philip Kane
Witches of Oz, Matthew & Julia Philips
Wondrous Land - The Faery Faith of Ireland by Dr Kay Mullin
Working With the Merlin, Geoff Hughes
Your Talking Pet, Ann Walker

# FREE detailed catalogue and FREE 'Inspiration' magazine

## Contact: Capall Bann Publishing, Auton Farm, Milverton, Somerset, TA4 1NE